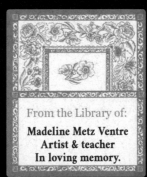

EUROPEAN ILLUSTRATION

The twelfth annual of European editorial, book, poster, advertising, design, animation and unpublished illustration.

Le douzième annuaire européen d'illustration de presse, du livre, de l'affiche, de publicité, du design, d'oeuvres non publiées et de film d'animation.

Der zöelfte Band des Jahrbuches 'European Illustration' über die Illustration auf redaktionellem Gebiet, im Buch, auf Plakat und Poster, in der Werbung, in unveröffentlichten Arbeiten, im Trickfilm und in der Gebrauchsgraphik.

European Illustration, 12 Carlton House Terrace, London SW1.

Book Design	*Buchdesign*
Carroll & Dempsey Limited	Carroll & Dempsey Limited
Designers	*Gestalter*
Mike Dempsey and Karen Wilks	Mike Dempsey and Karen Wilks
Cover, introduction and section break illustrations	*Ilustrationen fur Titelblatt, Einleitung und Zwischenblatter*
Karen Ludlow	Karen Ludlow
Annual Co-ordinators	*Produktions-Koordinatoren*
Maria Hodson and Julia Miller-Smith	Maria Hodson und Julia Miller-Smith

Printed in Japan by
Dai Nippon
Paper: 128GSM matt coated
Typeface: Garamond 3 Roman
& Garamond 3 Italic
Filmset by Metro Filmsetting

Published by Fleetbooks S.A.
Switzerland
Copyright © 1985

The following companies hold
exclusive trade distribution
rights for European
Illustration.
France: Sofedis, Paris
Brazil: Paulo Gorodetchi &
Cia Ltda, Sao Paulo
Spain: Commercial Atheneum,
Barcelona
USA/Canada: Harry N.
Abrams Inc., New York
UK: Columbus Books,
Bromley, Kent
Rest of the World: Fleetbooks
S.A., 100 Park Avenue,
New York, NY10017.
Direct Mail Rights:
UK and Europe:
Internos Books, Colville Road,
London W3 8BL.
USA: Print Bookstore,
6400 Goldsboro Road,
Bethesda, Maryland 20817.

Presentation du Livre	
Carroll & Dempsey Limited	
Mise en Page	
Mike Dempsey and Karen Wilks	
Illustrations pour la couverture, l'introduction et entre les sections	
Karen Ludlow	
Co-ordinatrices de la presentation	
Maria Hodson and Julia Miller-Smith	

Contents

This year, and perhaps more than ever before, the work in EUROPEAN ILLUSTRATION reflects a change I see in politics and lifestyles.

For the last few years we've seen a lot of work which has prided itself on its passion and, in some cases, its protest. The images of doom and gloom were everywhere.

Now, however, though the merchants of discord are still plying their trade, no-one seems to be in the market for their wares.

Andrzej Dudzinski, for example, whose images some may say are savage, is not represented here.

Other illustrators, whose ideas and techniques evoked a world in turmoil full of characters surviving chaos, are not to be seen either.

That's not to say, of course, that they have stopped work; that their particular form of protest has run out of steam. Far from it. The apocalyptic vision is still a force which guides the hands of artists everywhere.

What has happened – and this is reflected in the choices made by our AMERICAN ILLUSTRATION jury too – is that those who commission artwork for the media have shifted away towards a more decorative feel to the work they want. It's as if, sated with the kind of savage satire they have been so much concerned with just recently, they want only to present a calmer world.

It may be, of course, that today's art editors and art directors simply do not share the view of the world as a time bomb on a short fuse.

My own view is that many of them have come to terms with life as it is and, living and working in a more buoyant economic climate, they have decided to perpetrate what you'll see within these pages: a breath of optimism and, with it, a much enlarged EUROPEAN ILLUSTRATION annual.

I am indebted once again to Mike Dempsey for the design of this twelfth edition. His care over the presentation of our artists' work does them justice and confirms my belief that the work itself should always be seen to its best advantage.

If you would like to submit your work to next year's EUROPEAN ILLUSTRATION, you'll find a Call for Entries form enclosed. Entries must reach us by no later than February 20th, for selection during March. This is the pattern we follow every year and, in return for an entry fee of just £7.50, it offers you the opportunity to have your work displayed alongside the best of Europe's images, in the gallery that is EUROPEAN ILLUSTRATION.

In diesem Jahr, vielleicht mehr als je zuvor, reflektieren die Arbeiten in EUROPEAN ILLUSTRATION einen bemerkbaren Wandel in der Politik und im Lebensstil.

In den letzten Jahren haben wir viele Arbeiten gesehen, die stolz in ihrer Leidenschaft und manchmal in ihrem Protest waren. Ausdrücke des Untergangs und der Trübsal überall.

Heutzutage jedoch, obwohl die Händler der Zwietracht weiterhin ihren Handel betreiben, scheint niemand mehr deren Waren zu wollen.

Andrzej Dudzinski, zum Beispiel, dessen Arbeiten manche als grausam beschreiben mögen, ist hier nicht vertreten.

Andere Illustratoren, deren Ideen und technische Ausführungen eine Welt im Aufruhr hervorrufen, voll von Überlebenden des Chaos, sind ebenfalls nicht zu finden.

Das heißt natürlich nicht, daß sie nicht mehr arbeiten, daß ihre besondere Art des Protestes nicht mehr aktuell ist. Ganz im Gegenteil. Die apokalyptische Vorstellung hat weiterhin einen beträchtlichen Einfluß auf Künstler überall.

Der Wandel liegt darin – und dies reflektiert sich in der Auswahl, die von unserer AMERICAN ILLUSTRATION Jury getroffen wurde – daß diejenigen, die Illustrationen für die Medien in Auftrag geben, eher die mehr dekorativen Einflüsse in ihren Arbeiten suchen. Es ist als ob sie, übersättigt von der grausamen Satire, der sie vor kurzem ausgesetzt waren, nun eine ruhigere Welt beschreiben wollen.

Es mag natürlich sein, daß die heutigen Kunstredakteure und Kunstdirektoren einfach nicht die Auffassung teilen von einer Welt als Zeitbombe mit einem Kurzzünder.

Meine eigene Meinung ist, daß sich viele von ihnen mit dem heutigen Leben abgefunden haben und daß sie, durch ihre Arbeit in einem stabileren wirtschaftlichen Klima, entschlossen sind, das auszudrücken, was Sie auf diesen Seiten sehen: einen Hauch von Optimismus und, demzufolge, ein viel umfangreicheres EUROPEAN ILLUSTRATION Jahrbuch.

Dank bin ich wiederum Mike Dempsey schuldig für die Gestaltung dieser zwölften Ausgabe. Seine Sorgfalt bei der Wiedergabe der Arbeiten unserer Künstler wird ihnen gerecht und bestätigt mich in meinem Glauben, daß die Arbeiten selbst immer im besten Licht gesehen werden sollten.

Falls Sie daran interessiert sind, Ihre Arbeit für das nächste EUROPEAN ILLUSTRATION Jahrbuch einzureichen, finden Sie beiliegend ein Einsendeformular. Arbeiten sollten uns bis spätestens 20. Februar erreichen für die im März stattfindende Auswahl. Diese Einladung wiederholt sich jedes Jahr und gibt Ihnen die Möglichkeit, gegen eine Einsendegebühr von nur £7.50, Ihre Arbeiten neben den besten Europas auszustellen, in dem EUROPEAN ILLUSTRATION Schaukasten.

ette année peut-être plus que jamais auparavant, le travail dans EUROPEAN ILLUSTRATION reflète un changement que je constate en politique et en style de vie.

Au cours de ces dernières années j'ai vu bien des oeuvres qui se faisaient fort de montrer leur passion et, dans certains cas, leur protestation. Il n'y avait partout que des images de fatalité et de morbidité.

Maintenant, cependant, bien que les marchands de discorde exercent toujours leur métier, il ne semble plus y avoir de débouchés pour leurs marchandises.

Andrzej Dudzinski, par exemple, dont certains considèrent les imges comme sauvages, n'est pas représenté ici.

D'autres illustrateurs, dont les idées et les techniques évoquent un monde bouleversé plein de personnages survivant au chaos, ne s'y trouvent pas non plus.

Cela ne veut pas dire, bien sûr, qu'ils ont cessé de travailler, ni que leur forme particulière de protestation est arrivée à bout de souffle. Loin de là. La vision apocalyptique reste une force qui dirige la main d'artistes partout.

Ce qui s'est passé – et nous en voyons aussi le reflet dans les choix de notre jury de AMERICAN ILLUSTRATION – c'est que les responsables pour les commandes de travail artistique dans les médias ont dévié leurs orientations vers une touche plus décorative. C'est comme si, rassasiés par l'espèce de satire sauvage qui les a tant intéresser tout récemment, ils souhaitent désormais présenter un monde plus calme.

Il se peut, bien sûr, que les éditeurs artistiques et les directeurs artistiques d'aujourd'hui ne partagent tout simplement plus leur point de vue du monde comme une bombe à retardement sur le point d'exploser.

A mon sens nombre d'entre eux en sont venus à accepter la vie telle qu'elle est, et vivant et travaillant dans un climat économique plus stable, ont décidé de commettre ce que vous allez voir dans ces pages; un souffle d'optimisme, et de ce fait, un annuaire beaucoup plus grand de EUROPEAN ILLUSTRATION.

Une fois encore c'est à Mike Dempsey que je dois le design de cette douzième édition. Son soin de la présentation du travail d'artistes leur rend justice et me confirme dans mon opinion que le travail même doit toujours être présenté à son meilleur avantage.

Si vous souhaitez soumettre votre travail pour l'édition de EUROPEAN ILLUSTRATION de l'année prochaine, vous trouverez ci-inclus une invitation à concourir. Les demandes doivent nous parvenir au plus tard le 20 février, pour sélection en mars. C'est le mode que nous suivons tous les ans, et contre un droit de participation de £7.50, cela vous offre l'opportunité de voir votre travail exposé à côté des meilleurs images d'Europe, dans la galerie qu'est EUROPEAN ILLUSTRATION.

EDWARD BOOTH-CLIBBORN

BRIAN WEBB

Designer · Trickett & Webb Limited · London
Gestalter · Trickett & Webb Limited · London
Maquettiste · Trickett & Webb Limited · Londres

RITA MARSHALL

Art Director · Lausanne and New York
Art Direktor · Lausanne und New York
Directeur Artistique · Lausanne et New York

ALAIN WEILL

B.A. in Law and History of Art
Specialist in advertising and contemporary art · Paris
Rechtsanwalt, Diplom in Kunstgeschichte
Experte im Werbebereich und in zeitgenossischer Kunst · Paris
Licencie en droit – diplôme en histoire de l'art
Expert en art publicitaire et création contemporaine · Paris

JEANETTE COLLINS

Editorial Design Consultant · London
Redaktionelle Design-Beraterin · London
Conseiller de Mise en Pages · Londres

DEREK UNGLESS

Art Director · Rolling Stone · New York
Art Direktor · Rolling Stone · New York
Directeur Artistique · Rolling Stone · New York

MALCOLM GASKIN

Joint Creative Director · TBWA Limited · London
Mitverantwortlicher Kreativ-Direktor · TBWA Limited · London
Co-Directeur de Creation · TBWA Limited · London

B RIAN WEBB went to Liverpool and Canterbury schools of art. He spent four years working in London before meeting Lynn Trickett and founding their successful design group Trickett & Webb in 1971. The business is based on doing good work for interesting people, on growing without expanding – big enough to work for large corporations as well as little companies, but small enough for the founders to remain personally responsible for work. That work has won D&AD Silver Awards, been exhibited around the world and provided fun as well as profit for all concerned.

B RIAN WEBB hat an Kunstschulen in Liverpool und Canterbury studiert. Nach vier Jahren Tätigkeit in London traf er Lynn Trickett, und zusammen gründeten sie die erfolgreiche Design-Gruppe Trickett & Webb. Das Ziel der Gruppe ist, gute Arbeiten für interessante Kunden auszuführen und natürlich zu wachsen ohne Erweiterung – groß genug, um für große Organisationen wie auch kleine Firmen zu arbeiten, aber klein genug, daß die Gründer weiterhin persönlich in der Arbeit involviert sind. Ihre Arbeiten haben Silberpreise des D&AD gewonnen, sind überall in der Welt ausgestellt worden und haben für alle Beteiligten Spaß und auch Gewinn gebracht.

B RIAN WEBB a étudié aux écoles d'art de Liverpool et Canterbury. Il a passé quatre ans à travailler à Londres avant de rencontrer Lynn Trickett avec qui il a fondé leur groupe de design Trickett & Webb en 1971, groupe qui connaît un grand succès. L'affaire consiste à fournir un bon travail pour des personnes intéressantes, à s'agrandir sans s'étendre – assez grande pour travailler avec d'importantes corporations comme des compagnies plus restreintes, mais assez petite pour permettre aux fondateurs d'être personnellement responsables du travail. Ce travail a obtenu les prix d'argent de D&AD, a été exposé partout au monde et a fourni du plaisir ainsi que du bénéfice à tous les intéressés.

R ITA MARSHALL has been living in Lausanne, Switzerland for the last four years, designing and art directing books with Etienne Delessert. A series of twenty illustrated fairytales has just recently been published by Editions Grasset, Paris, Editions 24 Heures, Lausanne and Creative Education, Minneapolis. Previously she has worked as an art director for TBWA, Zurich and Tracy-Locke/BBD&O, Denver. She now lives in Connecticut with Delessert and together they are creating the first line of children's books for Rizzoli International in New York.

R ITA MARSHALL hat in den letzten vier Jahren in Lausanne gelebt und zusammen mit Etienne Delessert Bücher gestaltet. Eine Serie von zwanzig illustrierten Märchenbüchern ist vor kurzem von Editions Grasset, Paris, Editions 24 Heures, Lausanne und Creative Education, Minneapolis herausgegeben worden. Zuvor hat sie als Art Direktor für TBWA in Zürich und Tracy-Locke/ BBD&O in Denver gearbeitet. Heute lebt sie mit Delessert in Connecticut und gemeinsam gestalten sie die erste Kinderbuch-Reihe für Rizzoli International in New York.

R ITA MARSHALL a vécu à Lausanne, Suisse pendant quatre ans, s'occupant du design et de la direction artistique de livres avec Etienne Delessert. Une série de vingt contes de fées illustrés vient de paraître aux Editions Grasset à Paris, aux Editions 24 Heures à Lausanne, et à Creative Education, Minneapolis. Auparavant elle a travaillé comme directeur artistique chez TBWA, Zurich et Tracy-Loche/BBD&O, Denver. Elle vit actuellement au Connecticut avec Delessert et ils créent ensemble la première partie de livres d'enfants pour Rizzoli International de New York.

JEANETTE COLLINS hat Grafik an der Central School of Art and Design in London studiert. Sie arbeitete als Designer und Kunstredakteur für eine Reihe von Zeitschriften, wurde 1967 Art Direktor für die Frauenseiten der Times und 1970 Art Direktor der Times, worauf sie die Zeitung neu gestaltete. 1978 verließ sie die Times und gestaltete eine Reihe von neuen Publikationen, u.a. die Zeitschrift 'Now!' und vor kurzem 'Working Woman'. Sie hat Projekte ausgeführt für The New York Times, die Zeitung des Aga Khans in Nairobi, 'The Nation', und hat soeben einen Blindband für eine neue Frauenzeitschrift zusammengestellt, die in New York veröffentlicht werden soll. Jeanette Collins war zweimal Mitglied der European Illustration Jury, sowie Mitglied der D&AD Jury und des geschäftsführenden Ausschusses. Sie ist Mitglied der Royal Society of Arts.

JEANETTE COLLINS a étudié le design graphique à la Central School of Art and Design de Londres. Elle a travaillé pour un certain nombre de magazines comme designer et éditeur artistique avant d'entrer au Times en 1967 comme directeur artistique des pages féminines. En 1970 elle est devenue directeur artistique du Times et a changé l'aspect général du journal. Après avoir quitté The Times en 1978 Jeanette Collins a été designer et directeur artistique de plusieurs nouvelles publications dont "Now!" Magazine et tout récemment "Working Woman". Elle a travaillé à des projets pour le New York Times le journal de l'Aga Khan à Nairobi "The Nation" et elle vient de terminer la maquette d'un nouveau magazine féminin qui sera lancé à New York. Jeanette Collins a été membre deux fois du jury de European Illustration ainsi que membre du comité exécutif et du jury de D&AD. Elle est Associé (Fellow) de la Royal Society of Arts.

ALAIN WEILL was for several years the curator of the Poster Museum in Paris. He is now a consultant to various Government Agencies in France, a critic and a writer.

ALAIN WEILL war etliche Jahre Direktor des Plakat-Museums in Paris. Er ist heute Berater für verschiedene Regierungsstellen in Frankreich, Kritiker und Schriftsteller.

ALAIN WEILL a été pendant plusieurs années Conservateur du Musée de l'Affiche à Paris. Il est actuellement conseiller pour diverses agences gouvernementales en France, critique et écrivain.

JEANETTE COLLINS studied graphic design at London's Central School of Art and Design. She worked on a number of magazines as a designer and art editor before joining The Times in 1967 as Art Director of the Woman's pages. In 1970 she became Art Director of The Times, when she redesigned the paper. Since leaving The Times in 1978 Jeanette Collins has designed and art directed several new publications including 'Now!' Magazine and most recently 'Working Woman'. She has worked on projects for The New York Times, The Aga Khan's Nairobi newspaper 'The Nation' and has just completed a dummy for a new Woman's magazine to be launched in New York. Jeanette Collins has been a member of the European Illustration Jury twice as well as having been a member of the D&AD Executive Committee and Jury. She is a Fellow of the Royal Society of Arts.

DEREK UNGLESS was born in England and was a designer at Radio Times, the programme journal of the British Broadcasting Corporation. In 1978 he moved to Toronto, Canada and became Associate Art Director at Weekend Magazine. He moved to New York late in 1979 as Design Consultant for Esquire; returning six months later to Toronto, he became Art Director of Canada's oldest magazine, Saturday Night. He is presently living in New York City and is Art Director of ROLLING STONE. He has received numerous awards from, among others, The Design and Art Directors Club of Great Britain, the National Magazine Awards Foundation of Canada, and the Society of Publication Designers. He is on the committee of American Photography and he has lectured on magazine design in Canada and the USA.

DEREK UNGLESS, geborener Engländer, war Designer bei der Radio Times, Programmzeitschrift der British Broadcasting Corporation. 1978 zog er um nach Toronto, Kanada und wurde assoziierter Art Direktor des Weekend Magazine. Gegen Ende 1979 ging er nach New York as Designberater für Esquire, zog aber sechs Monate später zurück nach Toronto als Art Direktor der ältesten Zeitschrift Kanadas, Saturday Night. Zur Zeit lebt er in New York und ist Art Direktor von ROLLING STONE. Er hat etliche Preise gewonnen, u.a. die des Design und Art Directors Club of Great Britain, der National Magazine Awards Foundation of Canada und der Society of Publication Designers. Er ist Mitglied des Komitees von American Photography und hat Vorlesungen über Zeitschriftengestaltung in Kanada und den USA gehalten.

DEREK UNGLESS est né en Angleterre. Il a été designer au Radio Times, le journal programme de la British Broadcasting Corporation. En 1978 il est allé à Toronto, Canada pour devenir Directeur Artistique Adjoint à Weekend Magazine. Il est parti pour New York fin 1979 comme Design Conseil pour Esquire; puis est revenu six mois plus tard à Toronto, pour être Directeur artistique du plus ancien magazine du Canada, Saturday Night. Il vit actuellement à New York où il est Directeur artistique de ROLLING STONE. Il a reçu de nombreux prix en particulier du Design & Art Directors Club of Great Britain, le National Magazine Awards Foundation du Canada, et la Society of Publication Designers. Il fait partie du comité de American Photography et a donné des conférences sur le design de magazines au Canada et aux Etats Unis.

MALCOLM GASKIN qualified with a B.A. in Graphics from Manchester College of Art in 1973. He spent four years with Leo Burnett in London before joining TBWA in 1977, where he is the Joint Creative Director. During his career he has been responsible for several award winning advertising campaigns notably for Lego and for Nursing Recruitment.

MALCOLM GASKIN beendete sein Studium 1973 mit einer B.A. Auszeichnung in Grafik des Manchester College of Art. Er arbeitete vier Jahre lang bei Leo Burnett in London und ging 1977 nach TBWA, wo er heute mitverantwortlicher Kreativ-Direktor ist. Im Laufe seiner Karriere war er verantwortlich für mehrere preisgekrönte Werbekampagnen, insbesondere für Lego und die Anwerbung von Krankenschwestern.

MALCOLM GASKIN a obtenu une licence en Art Graphique du Manchester College of Art en 1973. Il a ensuite passé quatre ans avec Leo Burnett à Londres avant d'entrer à TBWA en 1977 où il est co-directeur de création. Au cours de sa carrière il a été responsable de plusieurs campagnes de publicité qui ont été récompensées de prix notamment celles de Lego et de Nursing Recruitment.

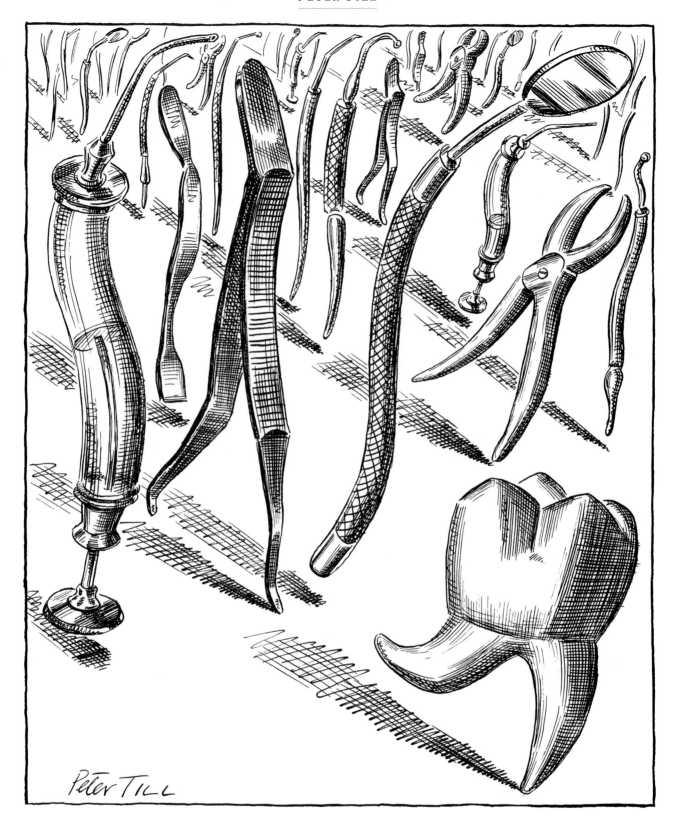

PēterTill

Art Director · Art Direktor · Directeur Artistique · David Driver

Publisher · Verlag · Editeur · Times Newspapers Limited

The Nation's Health	Die Gesundheit der Nation	La Santé de la Nation
For an article by Teresa Skelly	Für einen Artikel von Teresa	Pour un article de Teresa Skelly
in The Times 29th October	Skelly in The Times	dans The Times du 29 octobre
1984.	29. Oktober 1984.	1984.
Pen and ink in black	Feder und Tusche in	Plume et encre en noir
and white	schwarz-weiß	et blanc

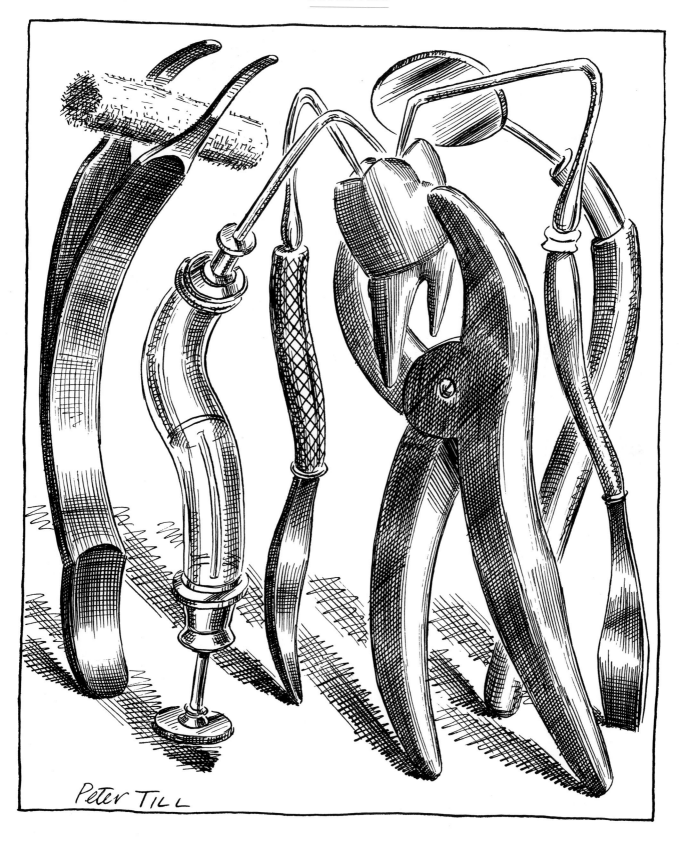

Peter Till

Art Director · Art Direktor · Directeur Artistique · David Driver

Publisher · Verlag · Editeur · Times Newspapers Limited

The Nation's Health
For an article by Teresa Skelly
in The Times 31st October
1984.
Pen and ink in black
and white

Die Gesundheit der Nation
Für einen Artikel von Teresa
Skelly in The Times
31. Oktober 1984.
Feder und Tusche in
schwarz-weiß

La Santé de la Nation
Pour un article de Teresa Skelly
dans The Times du 31 octobre
1984.
Plume et encre en noir
et blanc

Art Director · Art Direktor · Directeur Artistique · David Driver

Publisher · Verlag · Editeur · Times Newspapers Limited

The Nation's Health	Die Gesundheit der Nation	La Santé de la Nation
For an article by Teresa Skelly	Für einen Artikel von Teresa	Pour un article de Teresa Skelly
in The Times 1st November	Skelly in The Times	dans The Times du 1er
1984.	1. November 1984.	novembre 1984.
Pen and ink in black	Feder und Tusche in	Plume et encre en noir
and white	schwarz-weiß	et blanc

Art Editor · Kunstredakteur · Rédacteur Artistique · Martin Colyer

Publisher · Verlag · Editeur · BBC Publications

Lobbying – A New Act For
The Arts
Cover for an article by Malcolm
Davies in The Listener
14th February 1984.
Mixed media

Beeinflussung – eine neue
Aufgabe für die Kunstwelt
Titelblatt für einen Artikel von
Malcolm Davies in
The Listener 14. Februar 1984.
Mischtechnik

Groupe de pression – un
nouvel acte pour les Arts
Couverture pour un article de
Malcolm Davies dans The
Listener du 14 février 1984.
Moyens divers

Art Editor · Kunstredakteur · Rédacteur Artistique · Martin Colyer

Publisher · Verlag · Editeur · BBC Publications

Who's Afraid of Investigative Journalism? Cover for an article by Benjamin Wooley in The Listener 4th October 1984. Pen and ink and coloured pencil	Wer hat Angst vor untersuchendem Journalismus? Titelblatt für einen Artikel von Benjamin Wooley in The Listener 4. Oktober 1984. Feder und Tusche und Farbstifte	Qui a peur du journalisme d'investigation? Couverture pour un article de Benjamin Wooley dans The Listener du 4 octobre 1984. Plume et encre et crayon de couleur

Art Editor · Kunstredakteur · Rédacteur Artistique · Martin Colyer

Publisher · Verlag · Editeur · BBC Publications

| The Politics of the Thriller Cover for an article by Owen Dudley Edwards and John Sutherland in The Listener 21st June 1984. Acrylics | Die Politik der Detektivromane Titelblatt für einen Artikel von Owen Dudley Edwards und John Sutherland in The Listener 21. Juni 1984. Acryl | La politique du roman à suspense Couverture pour un article de Owen Dudley Edwards et John Sutherland dans The Listener du 21 juin 1984. Acryliques |

Art Director · Art Direktor · Directeur Artistique · Clive Crook

Designer · Gestalter · Maquettiste · David Ashmore

Publisher · Verlag · Editeur · The Observer Limited

Britons Observed:
Home Truths
Part 1 of an article by
Katharine Whitehorn and
Peter Kellner in The Observer
Magazine
16th September 1984.
Acrylics

Die Briten beobachtet:
Heim-Wahrheiten
Teil 1 eines Artikels von
Katharine Whitehorn und
Peter Kellner in The Observer
Magazine
16. September 1984.
Acryl

Les Anglais observés: quelques
vérités
1ère partie d'un article de
Katharine Whitehorn et Peter
Kellner dans The Observer
Magazine du 16 septembre
1984.
Acryliques

Art Director · Art Direktor · Directeur Artistique · Clive Crook

Designer · Gestalter · Maquettiste · David Ashmore

Publisher · Verlag · Editeur · The Observer Limited

| Britons Observed: Crime and Punishment Part 3 of an article by Katharine Whitehorn and Peter Kellner in The Observer Magazine 30th September 1984. Acrylics | Die Briten beobachtet: Verbrechen und Bestrafung Teil 3 eines Artikels von Katharine Whitehorn und Peter Kellner in The Observer Magazine 30. September 1984. Acryl | Les Anglais observés: Crime et Châtiment 3e partie d'un article de Katharine Whitehorn et Peter Kellner dans The Observer Magazine du 30 septembre 1984. Acryliques |

Designer · Gestalter · Maquettiste · Pedro Silmon

Publisher · Verlag · Editeur · Times Newspapers Limited

| For an article on 1945 vintage wine in The Sunday Times Colour Magazine September 1984. Acrylic and gouache | Für einen Artikel über Wein Jahrgang 1945 in The Sunday Times Colour Magazine September 1984. Acryl und Gouache | Pour un article sur le vin du millésime 1945 dans The Sunday Times Colour Magazine de septembre 1984. Acrylique et gouache |

Art Director · Art Direktor · Directeur Artistique · Janella Gibbs

Publisher · Verlag · Editeur · The Condé Nast Publications Ltd

Reproduced by kind permission of Vogue (c) Condé Nast Publications

The Aquarius Star Sign
For the Horoscope in Vogue
January 1985.
Ink in black and white

Das Sternzeichen Wassermann
Für das Horoskop in Vogue
Januar 1985.
Tusche in schwarz-weiß

Le signe astronomique du
Verseau
Pour l'horoscope dans Vogue
janvier 1985.
Encre en noir et blanc

Art Director · Art Direktor · Directeur Artistique · Derek Ungless

Designer · Gestalter · Maquettiste · Elizabeth Williams

Publisher · Verlag · Editeur · Rolling Stone

| 1984 Record Review For an article by Kurt Loder in Rolling Stone December 1984. Water-colour, ink and gouache | Plattenauswahl 1984 Für einen Artikel von Kurt Loder in Rolling Stone Dezember 1984. Wasserfarben, Tusche und Gouache | Compte rendu de disques 1984 Pour un article de Kurt Loder dans Rolling Stone décembre 1984. Aquarelle, encre et gouache |

Art Director · Art Direktor · Directeur Artistique · Roger Watt

Publisher · Verlag · Editeur · Paul Raymond Publications

The Effluent Society	Die Gesellschaft des Ausflusses	La société effluente
For The Done Thing, a regular feature in Men Only.	Für The Done Thing, eine Serie von Artikeln in Men Only.	Pour The Done Thing, article habituel dans Men Only.
Water-colour, ink and gouache	Wasserfarben, Tusche und Gouache.	Aquarelle, encre et gouache

Art Director · Art Direktor · Directeur Artistique · Derek Ungless

Designer · Gestalter · Maquettiste · Elizabeth Williams

Publisher · Verlag · Editeur · Rolling Stone

Culture Club sounds the alarm
For an article by Don Shewey
in Rolling Stone
11th November 1984.
Water-colour, ink and gouache

Culture Club gibt das
Alarmzeichen
Für einen Artikel von Don
Shewey in Rolling Stone
11. November 1984.
Wasserfarben, Tusche und
Gouache

Cri d'alarme du Culture Club
Pour un article de Don Shewey
dans Rolling Stone du
11 novembre 1984.
Aquarelle, encre et gouache

Art Director · Art Direktor · Directeur Artistique · Clive Crook

Designer · Gestalter · Maquettiste · Mary Hamlyn

Publisher · Verlag · Editeur · The Observer Limited

Spot of Bother	Kleine Schererei	Petit ennui
For an article in the Young	Für einen Artikel in Young	Pour un article dans le Young
Observer in The Observer	Observer in The Observer	Observer dans The Oberver
Magazine July 1984.	Magazine Juli 1984.	Magazine juillet 1984.
Water-colour, ink and gouache	Wasserfarben, Tusche und Gouache	Aquarelle, encre et gouache

Art Editor · Kunstredakteur · Directeur Artistique · Peter Derschka

Publisher · Verlag · Editeur · Vogel Verlag

Press Conferences	Presse Konferenzen	Conferences de presse
For an article by Heinz Bernutz in Management Wissen March 1985.	Für einen Artikel von Heinz Bernutz in Management Wissen März 1985.	Pour un article de Heinz Bernutz dans Management Wissen de mars 1985.
Acrylics and pastels	Acryl und Pastellfarben	Acryliques et pastels.

Art Editor · Kunstredakteur · Directeur Artistique · Peter Derschka

Publisher · Verlag · Editeur · Vogel Verlag

The Construction of Reality For an article by Fritz Raidt in Management Wissen February 1985. Acrylics and pastels	Die Konstruktion der Wirklichkeit Für einen Artikel von Fritz Raidt in Management Wissen Februar 1985. Acryl und Pastellfarben	La construction de la réalité Pour un article de Fritz Raidt dans Management Wissen de février 1985. Acryliques et pastels

Art Director · Art Direktor · Directeur Artistique · Bob Ciano

Designer · Gestalter · Maquettiste · Nora Sheehan

Publisher · Verlag · Editeur · Life Magazine Time Inc.

The Great Race (a)	Das große Rennen (a)	La grande course (a)
True Confessions (b)	Wahre Geständnisse (b)	Confessions Véritables (b)
For an article, Voices,	Für einen Artikel, Stimmen,	Pour un article, Voix, publié
published in Life Magazine	veröffentlicht in Life Magazine	dans Life Magazine en janvier
January 1985.	Januar 1985.	1985.
Mixed media	Mischtechnik	Moyens divers

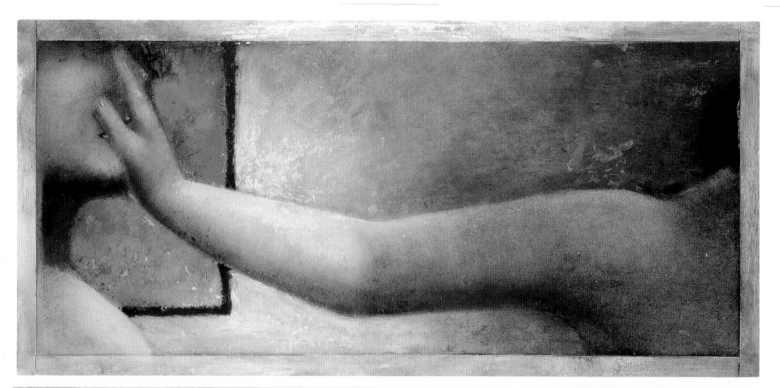

Art Director · Art Direktor · Directeur Artistique · Bob Ciano

Designer · Gestalter · Maquettiste · Nora Sheehan

Publisher · Verlag · Editeur · Life Magazine Time Inc.

Better Left Unsaid (a)
Fighting Words (b)
For an article, Voices,
published in Life Magazine
January 1985.
Mixed media

Lieber ungesagt lassen (a)
Kampfworte (b)
Für einen Artikel, Stimmen,
veröffentlicht in Life Magazine
Januar 1985.
Mischtechnik

Mieux vaut ne rien dire (a)
Mots combattants (b)
Pour un article, Voix, publié
dans Life Magazine 1985.
Moyens divers

Art Director · Art Direktor · Directeur Artistique · Bob Ciano

Designer · Gestalter · Maquettiste · Nora Sheehan

Publisher · Verlag · Editeur · Life Magazine Time Inc.

Money Talks (a)	Geld redet (a)	Questions d'argent (a)
Crime and Punishment (b)	Verbrechen und Strafe (b)	Crime et châtiment (b)
For an article, Voices,	Für einen Artikel, Stimmen,	Pour un article, Voix, publié
published in Life Magazine	veröffentlicht in Life Magazine	dans Life Magazine en janvier
January 1985.	Januar 1985.	1985.
Mixed media	Mischtechnik	Moyens divers

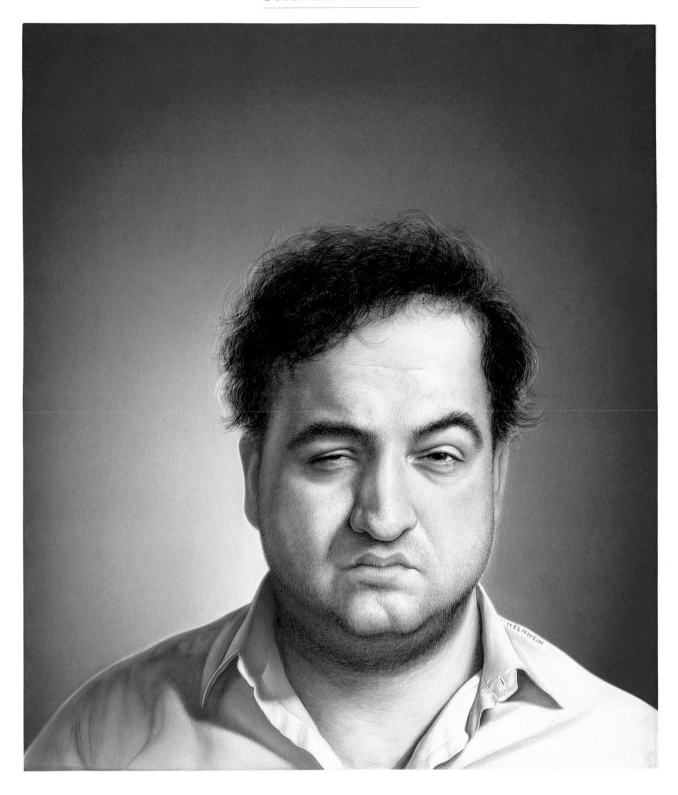

Art Director · Art Direktor · Directeur Artistique · Derek Ungless

Publisher · Verlag · Editeur · Rolling Stone

John Belushi's Troubled Sleep For an article by Lynn Hirshberg in Rolling Stone September 27th 1984. Gouache	John Belushis unruhiger Schlaf Für einen Artikel von Lynn Hirshberg in Rolling Stone 27. September 1984. Gouache	Sommeil agité de John Belushi Pour un article de Lynn Hirshberg dans Rolling Stone 27 septembre 1984. Gouache

Laughter is good medicine.

Art Editor · Kunstredakteur · Rédacteur Artistique · Mickey Soutendijk

Publisher · Verlag · Editeur · The Condé Nast Publications Ltd

Laughter is good medicine For an article by Susan Lang in Vogue December 1984. Water-colour and ink	Lachen ist gute Medizin Für einen Artikel von Susan Lang in Vogue Dezember 1984. Wasserfarben und Tusche	Rire est de la bonne médecine Pour un article de Susan Lang dans Vogue de décembre 1984. Aquarelle et encre

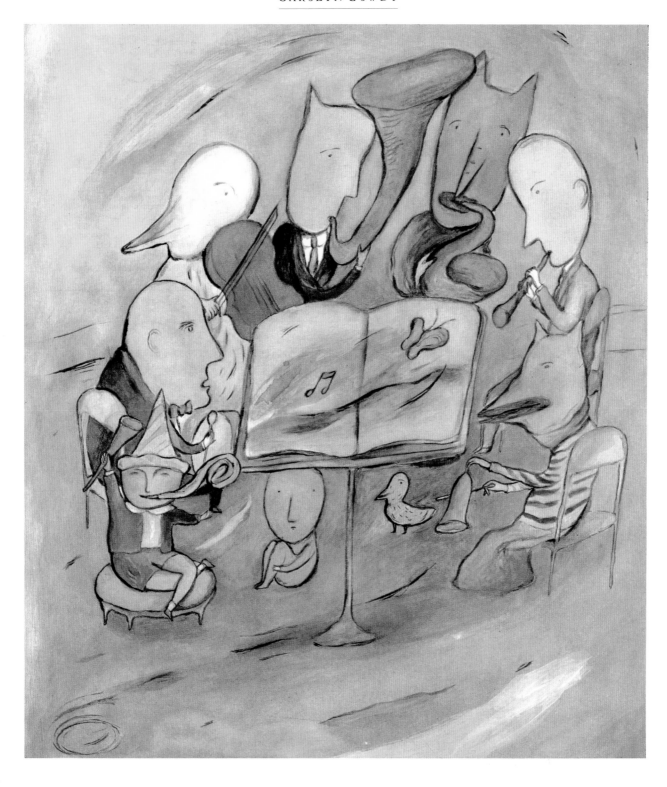

Art Director · Art Direktor · Directeur Artistique · Joanne Barber

Designer · Gestalter · Maquettiste · Joanne Barber

Publisher · Verlag · Editeur · Rhinegold Publishing

Educating the Community
For an article by Robert
Maycock in Classical Music
June 1984.
Water-colour and ink

Die Erziehung der
Allgemeinheit
Für einen Artikel von Robert
Maycock in Classical Music
Juni 1984.
Wasserfarben und Tusche

Education de la communauté
Pour un article de Robert
Maycock dans Classical Music
du juin 1984.
Aquarelle et encre

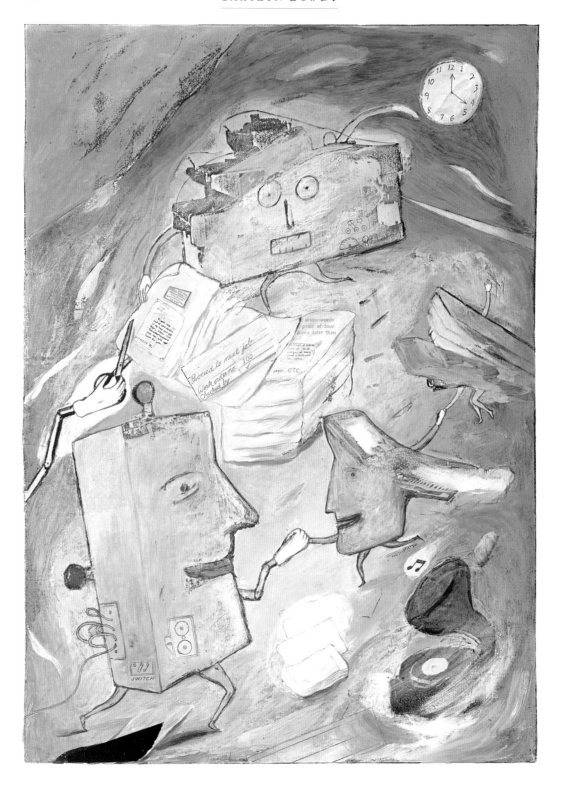

Art Director · Art Direktor · Directeur Artistique · John Clements

Designer · Gestalter · Maquettiste · John Clements

Publisher · Verlag · Editeur · Benn Publications

Inline or Offline?
For an article by Caryl Holland
in Printing World May 1984.
Water-colour, ink and collage

Mit oder ohne Beigerät?
Für einen Artikel von Caryl
Holland in Printing World
Mai 1984.
Wasserfarben, Tusche und
Collage

Sous-programme ou en
autonome?
Pour un article de Caryl
Holland dans Printing World
de mai 1984.
Aquarelle, encre et collage

Art Director · Art Direktor · Directeur Artistique · Richard Hartnell

Publisher · Verlag · Editeur · Royal College of Nursing

A Pain in the Back
For an article by Laura
Swaffield in Lampada
September 1984.
Water-colour, ink and collage

Rückenschmerzen
Für einen Artikel von Laura
Swaffield in Lampada
September 1984.
Wasserfarben, Tusche und
Collage

Une douleur dans le dos
Pour un article de Laura
Swaffield dans Lampada de
septembre 1984.
Aquarelle, encre et college

Art Director · Art Direktor · Directeur Artistique · Hans-Georg Pospischil

Publisher · Verlag · Editeur · Frankfurter Allgemeine Zeitung GmbH

The Moon Has Risen	Der Mond ist aufgegangen	La lune s'est levée
For an article by Siegfried	Für einen Artikel von Siegfried	Pour un article de Siegfried
Diehl in Frankfurter	Diehl in Frankfurter	Diehl dans Frankfurter
Allgemeine Magazin	Allgemeine Magazin	Allgemeine Magazin
12th October 1984.	12. Oktober 1984.	12 octobre 1984.
Mixed media	Mischtechnik	Moyens divers

Art Director · Art Direktor · Directeur Artistique · Hans-Georg Pospischil

Publisher · Verlag · Editeur · Frankfurter Allgemeine Zeitung GmbH

The Moon Has Risen
For an article by Siegfried
Diehl in Frankfurter
Allgemeine Magazin
12th October 1984.
Mixed media

Der Mond ist aufgegangen
Für einen Artikel von Siegfried
Diehl in Frankfurter
Allgemeine Magazin
12. Oktober 1984.
Mischtechnik

La lune s'est levée
Pour un article de Siegfried
Diehl dans Frankfurter
Allgemeine Magazin
12 octobre 1984.
Moyens divers

Art Director · Art Direktor · Directeur Artistique · Hans-Georg Pospischil

Publisher · Verlag · Editeur · Frankfurter Allgemeine Zeitung GmbH

Crickets and Ants	Von Grillen und Ameisen	Grillons et fourmis
For an article by Dietmar	Für einen Artikel von Dietmar	Pour un article de Dietmar
Polaczek in Frankfurter	Polaczek in Frankfurter	Polaczek dans Frankfurter
Allgemeine Magazin	Allgemeine Magazin	Allgemeine Magazin
16th March 1984.	16. März 1984.	16 mars 1984.
Mixed media	Mischtechnik	Moyens divers

Art Director · Art Direktor · Directeur Artistique · Hans-Georg Pospischil

Publisher · Verlag · Editeur · Frankfurter Allgemeine Zeitung GmbH

Crickets and Ants	Von Grillen und Ameisen	Grillons et fourmis
For an article by Dietmar	Für einen Artikel von Dietmar	Pour un article de Dietmar
Polaczek in Frankfurter	Polaczek in Frankfurter	Polaczek dans Frankfurter
Allgemeine Magazin	Allgemeine Magazin	Allgemeine Magazin
16th March 1984.	16. März 1984.	16 mars 1984.
Mixed media	Mischtechnik.	Moyens divers

Art Director · Art Direktor · Directeur Artistique · Hans-Georg Pospischil

Publisher · Verlag · Editeur · Frankfurter Allgemeine Zeitung GmbH

Crickets and Ants	Von Grillen und Ameisen	Grillons et fourmis
For an article by Dietmar	Für einen Artikel von Dietmar	Pour un article de Dietmar
Polaczek in Frankfurter	Polaczek in Frankfurter	Polaczek dans Frankfurter
Allgemeine Magazin	Allgemeine Magazin	Allgemeine Magazin
16th March 1984.	16. März 1984.	16 mars 1984.
Mixed media	Mischtechnik	Moyens divers

Art Director · Art Direktor · Directeur Artistique · Hans-Georg Pospischil

Publisher · Verlag · Editeur · Frankfurter Allgemeine Zeitung GmbH

Crickets and Ants	Von Grillen und Ameisen	Grillons et fourmis
For an article by Dietmar	Für einen Artikel von Dietmar	Pour un article de Dietmar
Polaczek in Frankfurter	Polaczek in Frankfurter	Polaczek dans Frankfurter
Allgemeine Magazin	Allgemeine Magazin	Allgemeine Magazin
16th March 1984.	16. März 1984.	16 mars 1984.
Mixed media	Mischtechnik	Moyens divers

Art Director · Art Direktor · Directeur Artistique · Hans-Georg Pospischil

Publisher · Verlag · Editeur · Frankfurter Allgemeine Zeitung GmbH

Crickets and Ants	Von Grillen und Ameisen	Grillons et fourmis
For an article by Dietmar	Für einen Artikel von Dietmar	Pour un article de Dietmar
Polaczek in Frankfurter	Polaczek in Frankfurter	Polaczek dans Frankfurter
Allgemeine Magazin	Allgemeine Magazin	Allgemeine Magazin
16th March 1984.	16. März 1984.	16 mars 1984.
Mixed media	Mischtechnik	Moyens divers

Art Director · Kunstredakteur · Directeur Artistique · Margaret Donagan

Publisher · Verlag · Editeur · Pharos Publications Limited

Antennae	Antennen	Antennes
World of Interiors	World of Interiors	World of Interiors
September 1984.	September 1984.	septembre 1984.
Water-colour and ink	Wasserfarben und Tusche	Aquarelle et encre

Art Director · Art Direktor · Directeur Artistique · Clive Crook

Designer · Gestalter · Maquettiste · Mary Hamlyn

Publisher · Verlag · Editeur · The Observer Limited

On the Write Track
The Observer Magazine
9th December 1984.
Ink in black and white

Auf dem richtigen
Schreib-Weg
The Observer Magazine
9. Dezember 1984.
Tusche in schwarz-weiß

En piste d'écriture
The Observer Magazine
9 décembre 1984.
Encre en noir et blanc

Art Director · Art Direktor · Directeur Artistique · Clive Crook

Designer · Gestalter · Maquettiste · Debi Angel

Publisher · Verlag · Editeur · The Observer Limited

Children's Toy Innovators
For an article by Sue Arnold in
The Observer Magazine
16th December 1984.
Ink in black and white

Die Erfinder von
Kinderspielzeugen
Für einen Artikel von Sue
Arnold in The Observer
Magazine
16. Dezember 1984.
Tusche in schwarz-weiß

Innovateurs de jouets d'enfants
Pour un article de Sue Arnold
dans The Observer Magazine
16 décembre 1984.
Encre en noir et blanc

-Don't shoot the pianola·The bishop and the bucket·Frost in the shrubbery·The comet connection·Leading by the nose?·Fire of the Lord-

Art Editor · Kunstredakteur · Redacteur Artistique · Chris Jones

Publisher · Verlag · Editeur · IPC Magazines Limited

Christmas Cover
For New Scientist
20th December 1984.
Scraperboard and water-colour

Weihnachts-Titelblatt
Für New Scientist
20. Dezember 1984.
Schabtechnik und
Wasserfarben

Couverture de Noël
Pour New Scientist du
20 décembre 1984.
Carte grattage at aquarelle

Art Director · Art Direktor · Directeur Artistique · Mike Lackersteen

Publisher · Verlag · Editeur · Redwood Publishing

The Shape of Cars to Come
For an article by Clive Jacobs
in Expression November 1984.
Scraperboard and water-colour

Die Form zukünftiger Autos
Für einen Artikel von Clive
Jacobs in Expression
November 1984.
Schabtechnik und
Wasserfarben

La forme des voitures de
l'avenir
Pour un article de Clive Jacobs
dans Expression de novembre
1984.
Carte grattage et aquarelle

Art Director · Art Direktor · Directeur Artistique · Colin McHenry

Publisher · Verlag · Editeur · National Magazines

24 Hour London	London – 24 Stunden lang	Les vingt quatre heures de
For various articles on London	Für verschiedene Artikel über	Londres
in Good Housekeeping	London in Good Housekeeping	Pour divers articles sur Londres
September 1984.	September 1984.	dans Good Housekeeping de
Scraperboard and water-colour	Schabtechnik und	septembre 1984.
	Wasserfarben	Carte grattage et aquarelle

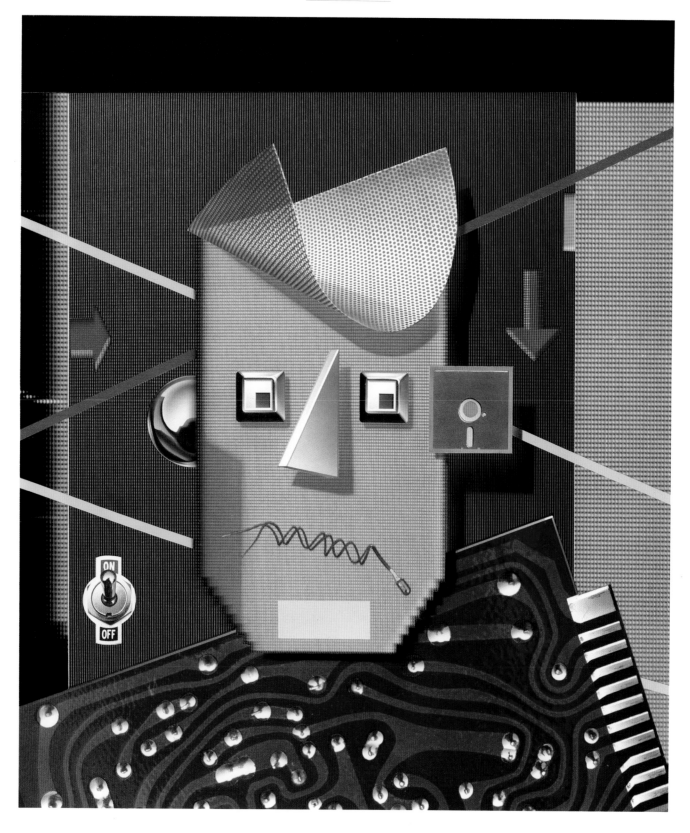

Art Director · Art Direktor · Directeur Artistique · Clive Crook

Designer · Gestalter · Maquettiste · Mary Hamlyn

Publisher · Verlag · Editeur · The Observer Limited

Technology Extra
Cover for The Observer
Magazine
15th April 1984.
Photo montage and airbrush

Technologie-Beilage
Titelblatt für The Observer
Magazine
15. April 1984.
Fotomontage und
Spritztechnik

Technologie extra
Couverture pour The Observer
Magazine
15 avril 1984.
Photo montage et aérographe

Art Director · Art Direktor · Directeur Artistique · John Tennant
Publisher · Verlag · Editeur · Times Newspapers Limited

Making Chocolate Truffles	Die Zubereitung von	Confection de truffes au
For an article by	Schokoladentrüffeln	chocolat
Loyd Grossman	Für einen Artikel von	Pour un article de
in The Sunday Times	Loyd Grossman	Loyd Grossman
Colour Magazine	in The Sunday Times	dans The Sunday Times
7th October 1984.	Colour Magazine	Colour Magazine
Collage and water-colour	7. Oktober 1984.	7 octobre 1984.
	Collage und Wasserfarben	Collage et aquarelle

Art Director · Art Direktor · Directeur Artistique · Jean-Jacques Hauwy

Publisher · Verlag · Editeur · L'Express

Story of Bread	Die Geschichte des Brotes	Histoire de Pains
For a short story by	Für eine Kurzgeschichte von	Pour une nouvelle de
Michel Tournier	Michel Tournier	Michel Tournier
in L'Express December 1984.	in L'Express Dezember 1984.	dans L'Express de décembre
Pen and ink and gouache	Feder und Tusche und	1984.
	Gouache	Plume et encre et gouache

Art Director · Art Direktor · Directeur Artistique · Clive Crook

Designer · Gestalter · Maquettiste · Graham Mitchener

Publisher · Verlag · Editeur · The Observer Limited

Flying Bottles	Fliegende Flaschen	Bouteilles volantes
For Wine Extra in The	Für Wine Extra in The	Pour Wine Extra dans The
Observer Magazine	Observer Magazine	Observer Magazine
18th November 1984.	18. November 1984.	18 novembre 1984.
Gouache	Gouache	Gouache

Art Director · Art Direktor · Directeur Artistique · Clive Crook

Designer · Gestalter · Maquettiste · Graham Mitchener

Publisher · Verlag · Editeur · The Observer Limited

Waiter with Tray	Kellner mit Tablett	Garçon au plateau
For Wine Extra in The	Für Wine Extra in The	Pour Wine Extra dans The
Observer Magazine	Observer Magazine	Observer Magazine
18th November 1984.	18. November 1984.	18 novembre 1984.
Gouache	Gouache	Gouache

Art Director · Art Direktor · Directeur Artistique · Clive Crook

Designer · Gestalter · Maquettiste · Graham Mitchener

Publisher · Verlag · Editeur · The Observer Limited

Wine Glass Book	Das Weinglas-Buch	Livre sur les verres à vin
For Wine Extra in The	Für Wine Extra in The	Pour Wine Extra dans The
Observer Magazine	Observer Magazine	Observer Magazine
18th November 1984.	18. November 1984.	18 novembre 1984.
Gouache	Gouache	Gouache

Art Director · Art Direktor · Directeur Artistique · John Tennant

Publisher · Verlag · Editeur · Times Newspapers Limited

Travel: South Sea Bauble For an article by Mark Ottaway in The Sunday Times Colour Magazine 21st October 1984. Acrylics	Reisen: Südsee-Perle Für einen Artikel von Mark Ottaway in The Sunday Times Colour Magazine 21. Oktober 1984. Acryl	Voyage: babiole des Mers du Sud Pour un article de Mark Ottaway dans The Sunday Times Colour Magazine 21 octobre 1984. Acryliques

Art Director · Art Direktor · Directeur Artistique · Denise Barnes

Publisher · Verlag · Editeur · National Magazine Company

My Name is John.
I'm an alcoholic
For an article by
John Trevithick
in Cosmopolitan April 1985.
Acrylics

Mein Name ist John.
Ich bin ein Alkoholiker
Für einen Artikel von
John Trevithick
in Cosmopolitan April 1985.
Acryl

Je m'appelle John.
Je suis alcoolique
Pour un article de
John Trevithick
dans Cosmopolitan d'avril
1985.
Acryliques

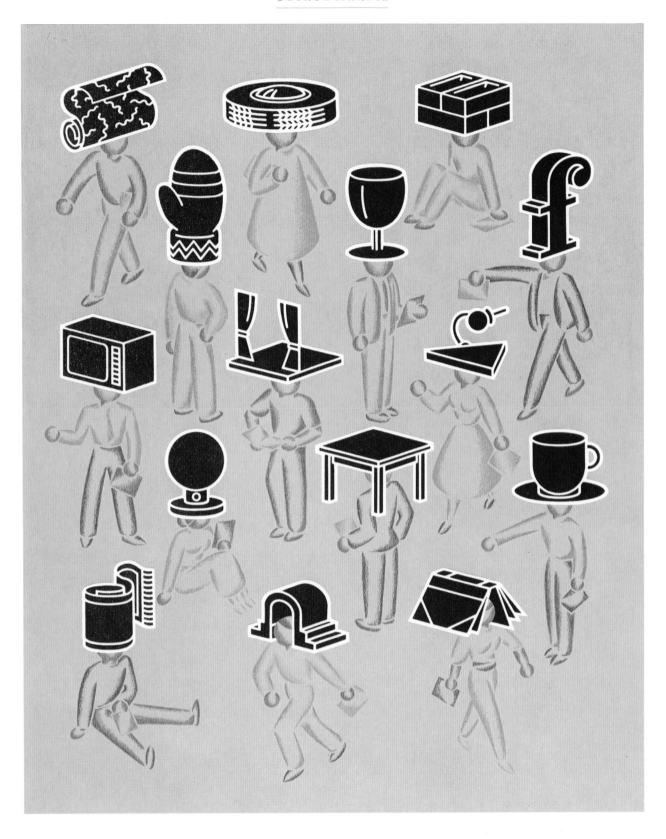

Art Director · Art Direktor · Directeur Artistique · Alastair Best ·

Publisher · Verlag · Editeur · S.I.A.D.

Cover for Designer Magazine	Titelblatt für Designer	Couverture pour Designer
July/August 1984.	Magazine	Magazine
Crayon and ink	Juli/August 1984.	juillet/août 1984.
	Farbstifte und Tusche	Pastel et encre

Art Director · Art Direktor · Directeur Artistique · John Tennant

Designer · Gestalter · Maquettiste · Gilvrie Misstear

Publisher · Verlag · Editeur · Times Newspapers Limited

ABC Diet and Body Plan: Behaviour For an article by Oliver Gillie and Suzane Raby in The Sunday Times Colour Magazine 10th June 1984. Pastel over gouache	ABC Diät- und Körperplanung: Auftreten Für einen Artikel von Oliver Gillie und Suzane Raby in The Sunday Times Colour Magazine 10. Juni 1984. Pastellfarben über Gouache	ABC Programme de diététique et de remise en forme: comportement Pour un article d'Oliver Gillie et Suzane Raby dans The Sunday Times Colour Magazine 10 juin 1984. Pastel sur gouache

Art Editor · Kunstredakteur · Rédacteur Artistique · April Silver

Publisher · Verlag · Editeur · Esquire Associates

Redemption Songs	Lieder der Befreiung	Chansons de rédemption
For an article by Bob Shacochis	Für einen Artikel von	Pour un article de
in Esquire March 1984.	Bob Shacochis	Bob Shacochis
Pastels	in Esquire März 1984.	dans Esquire de mars 1984.
	Pastellfarben	Pastels

Art Director · Art Direktor · Directeur Artistique · Hans-Georg Pospischil

Publisher · Verlag · Editeur · Frankfurter Allgemeine Zeitung GmbH

Weather	Wetter	Le Temps
For an article by	Für einen Artikel von	Pour un article
Eckhard Henscheid	Eckhard Henscheid	d'Eckhard Henscheid
in Frankfurter Allgemeine	in Frankfurter Allgemeine	dans Frankfurter Allgemeine
Magazin	Magazin	Magazin
19th April 1984.	19. April 1984.	19 avril 1984.
Cut paper, coloured pencils,	Geschnittenes Papier,	Découpage, crayons de
Pantone paper	Farbstifte, Pantone Papier	couleur, papier Pantone

Art Director · Art Direktor · Directeur Artistique · Hans-Georg Pospischil

Publisher · Verlag · Editeur · Frankfurter Allgemeine Zeitung GmbH

Dealing with Personal Computers For an article in Frankfurter Allgemeine Magazin 30th March 1984. Gouache	Über den Umgang mit Personal-Computern Für einen Artikel in Frankfurter Allgemeine Magazin 30. März 1984. Gouache	De l'utilisation des micro-ordinateurs Pour un article dans Frankfurter Allgemeine Magazin 30 mars 1984. Gouache

Art Director · Art Direktor · Directeur Artistique · Clive Crook

Designer · Gestalter · Maquettiste · Debi Angel

Publisher · Verlag · Editeur · The Observer Limited

Fishyssoise	Fishyssoise	Soupe au poisson
For an article by Jane Grigson	Für einen Artikel von	Pour un article de Jane Grigson
in The Observer Magazine	Jane Grigson	dans The Observer Magazine
3rd March 1984.	in The Observer Magazine	du 3 mars 1984.
Water-colour	3. März 1984.	Aquarelle
	Wasserfarben	

Art Editor · Kunstredakteur · Rédacteur Artistique · Sue Tritton

Publisher · Verlag · Editeur · V.N.U. Business Publications

Play Your Cards Right
For an article by Neville Ash
in Commodore Answers
November 1984.
Pencils

Spielen Sie Ihre Karten richtig
Für einen Artikel von
Neville Ash
in Commodore Answers
November 1984.
Bleistift

Jouez bien vos cartes
Pour un article de Neville Ash
dans Commodore Answers de
novembre 1984.
Crayon

Art Editor · Kunstredakteur · Rédacteur Artistique · Martin Richardson

Designer · Gestalter · Maquettiste · Sue Miller

Publisher · Verlag · Editeur · IPC Magazines Limited

Blind Spots
Woman's Own 27th April
1984.
Pencils

Blindpunkte
Woman's Own 27. April
1984.
Bleistift

Points morts
Woman's Own 27 avril 1984.
Crayons

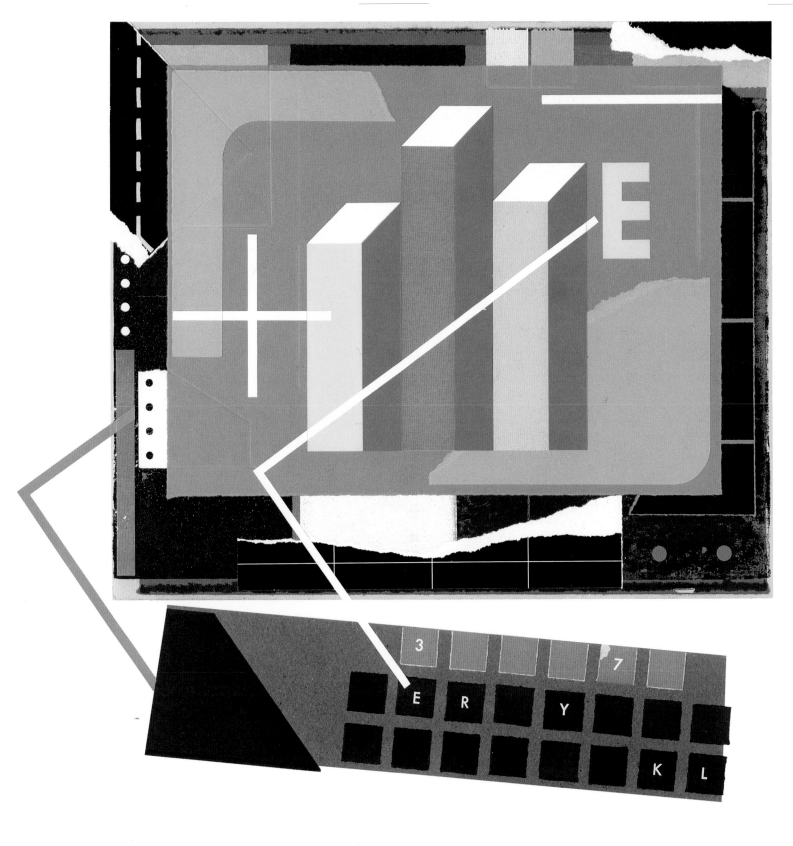

Art Director · Art Direktor · Directeur Artistique · Clive Crook

Designer · Gestalter · Maquettiste · Mary Hamlyn

Publisher · Verlag · Editeur · The Observer Limited

Technology Extra
The Observer Magazine
15th April 1984.
Collage

Technologie-Beilage
The Observer Magazine
15. April 1984.
Collage

Technologie-Spécial
The Observer Magazine
15 avril 1984.
Collage

Art Director · Art Direktor · Directeur Artistique · Christa Feldmann

Publisher · Verlag · Editeur · Times Newspapers Limited

The Young Divorcees
For an article by Cornelia Kazis
and Yvonne Reck in Voilà
September 1984.
Mixed media

Die jungen Geschiedenen
Für einen Artikel von
Cornelia Kazis
und Yvonne Reck in Voilà!
September 1984.
Mischtechnik

Les Jeunes Divorcés
Pour un article de
Cornelia Kazis et
Yvonne Reck dans Voilà de
septembre 1984.
Moyens divers

Art Director · Art Direktor · Directeur Artistique · Claire Whiddon

Designer · Gestalter · Maquettiste · Brian Goodall

Publisher · Verlag · Editeur · The North Sea Sun Oil Company

Overall System Concept in Phase One Balmoral July 1984. Airbrush and mixed media	Das gesamte System-Konzept in Phase One Balmoral Juli 1984. Spritztechnik und Mischtechnik	Concept de système global dans Phase One Balmoral juillet 1984 Aérographe et moyens divers

Art Director · Art Direktor · Directeur Artistique · Clive Crook

Publisher · Verlag · Editeur · The Observer Limited

An Annual Event	Ein jährliches Ereignis	Un événement annuel
The Observer Magazine	The Observer Magazine	The Observer Magazine
4th March 1984.	4. März 1984.	4 mars 1984.
Acrylics	Acryl	Acryliques

Art Director · Art Direktor · Directeur Artistique · April Silver

Publisher · Verlag · Editeur · Esquire Associates

The Hair of the Beast For a short story by Tom Robbins in Esquire November 1984. Gouache	Das Haar der Bestie Für eine Kurzgeschichte von Tom Robbins in Esquire November 1984. Gouache	Le poil de la bête Pour une nouvelle de Tom Robbins dans Esquire novembre 1984. Gouache

The Little Match Girl

As the Dusk gathers on *Christmas Day*, a Little Match Girl stands in the snow.....

The soft flakes fall from the sky like *goose feathers*......

Behind *double-glazing*, coloured lights *blink*...and *blink* in supplication......

...The Little Match Girl presses her tiny nose up against the cold glass....

...and peers inside...

...And her warm heart *melts* with *sorrow* for the *poor*, costive folk within.....

Publisher · Verlag · Editeur · The Observer Limited

Little Match Girl
The Observer Magazine
23rd December 1984.
Mixed media

Das kleine Streichholzmädchen
The Observer Magazine
23. Dezember 1984.
Mischtechnik

La petite fille aux allumettes
The Observer Magazine
23 décembre 1984.
Moyens divers

Publisher · Verlag · Editeur · The Observer Limited

Little Match Girl	Das kleine Streichholzmädchen	La petite fille aux allumettes
The Observer Magazine	The Observer Magazine	The Observer Magazine
23rd December 1984.	23. Dezember 1984.	23 décembre 1984.
Mixed media	Mischtechnik	Moyens divers

How *lovely* to bring **JOY** back to a tiny face!

And, although these deserving folk are rich, they are also *honest* ....and very, very grateful....

But the worthy folk insist. They give the Little Match Girl all they can spare : *modest, simple gifts* .....

And this Act of Gratitude kindles a Cheery Glow in all their hearts.....

A Desk Diary

Lurex Leg Warmers

some vivid **Bath Salts**

An executive's battery-operated **Mulling Poker** *(personalised)*

© Posy Simmonds

Publisher · Verlag · Editeur · The Observer Limited

Little Match Girl	Das kleine Streichholzmädchen	La petite fille aux allumettes
The Observer Magazine	The Observer Magazine	The Observer Magazine
23rd December 1984.	23. Dezember 1984.	23 décembre 1984.
Mixed media	Mischtechnik	Moyens divers

Art Director · Art Direktor · Directeur Artistique · John Tennant

Publisher · Verlag · Editeur · Times Newspapers Limited

Life After Life
For an article by Tony Parker
in The Sunday Times Colour
Magazine
24th March 1985.
Water-colour, pencil and
graphite

Leben nach der Lebensstrafe
Für einen Artikel von
Tony Parker
in The Sunday Times Colour
Magazine
24. März 1985.
Wasserfarben, Bleistift und
Graphit

La vie au delà de la vie
Pour un article de Tony Parker
dans The Sunday Times Colour
Magazine
24 mars 1985.
Aquarelle, crayon et mine de
plomb

Art Director · Art Direktor · Directeur Artistique · Bush Hollyhead

Photographer · Photograph · Photographe · James Stewart

Publisher · Verlag · Editeur · Seibundo Shinkosha Publishing Company Limited

NTA Studios	NTA Studios	Studios NTA
Cover for Idea Magazine	Titelblatt für Idea Magazine	Couverture pour Idea Magazine
April 1985.	April 1985.	avril 1985.
Papier mâché and collage	Papiermâché und Collage	Papier mâché et collage

Art Director · Art Direktor · Directeur Artistique · Ian Craig

Publisher · Verlag · Editeur · Jonathan Cape Limited

The Bee On The Comb	Die Biene auf der Wabe	L'Abeille sur ses rayons de miel
Illustrations from the book by	Illustrationen aus dem Buch	Illustrations du livre par
Kit Williams.	von Kit Williams.	Kit Williams.
Oil on Canvas	Öl auf Leinwand	Huile sur toile

Art Director · Art Direktor · Directeur Artistique · Ian Craig

Publisher · Verlag · Editeur · Jonathan Cape Limited

The Bee On The Comb	Die Biene auf der Wabe	L'Abeille sur ses rayons de miel
Illustrations from the book by	Illustrationen aus dem Buch	Illustrations du livre par
Kit Williams.	von Kit Williams.	Kit Williams.
Oil on Canvas	Öl auf Leinwand	Huile sur toile

Art Director · Art Direktor · Directeur Artistique · Ian Craig

Publisher · Verlag · Editeur · Jonathan Cape Limited

The Bee On The Comb	Die Biene auf der Wabe	L'Abeille sur ses rayons de miel
Illustrations from the book by	Illustrationen aus dem Buch	Illustrations du livre par
Kit Williams.	von Kit Williams.	Kit Williams.
Oil on Canvas	Öl auf Leinwand	Huile sur toile

Art Director · Art Direktor · Directeur Artistique · Etienne Delessert

Designer · Gestalter · Maquettiste · Rita Marshall

Publisher · Verlag · Editeur · Editions 24 Heures

Rose Blanche
A book by Roberto Innocenti
and Christophe Gallaz
published in March 1985.
Water-colour

Weiße Rose
Ein Buch von
Roberto Innocenti und
Christophe Gallaz
herausgegeben im März 1985.
Wasserfarben

Rose Blanche
Livre de Roberto Innocenti et
Christophe Gallaz
publié en mars 1985.
Aquarelle

Art Director · Art Direktor · Directeur Artistique · Etienne Delessert

Designer · Gestalter · Maquettiste · Rita Marshall

Publisher · Verlag · Editeur · Editions 24 Heures

Rose Blanche
A book by Roberto Innocenti
and Christophe Gallaz
published in March 1985.
Water-colour

Weiße Rose
Ein Buch von
Roberto Innocenti und
Christophe Gallaz
herausgegeben im März 1985.
Wasserfarben

Rose Blanche
Livre de Roberto Innocenti et
Christophe Gallaz
publié en mars 1985.
Aquarelle

Art Director · Art Direktor · Directeur Artistique · Etienne Delessert

Designer · Gestalter · Maquettiste · Rita Marshall

Publisher · Verlag · Editeur · Editions 24 Heures

Rose Blanche
A book by Roberto Innocenti
and Christophe Gallaz
published in March 1985.
Water-colour

Weiße Rose
Ein Buch von
Roberto Innocenti und
Christophe Gallaz
herausgegeben im März 1985.
Wasserfarben

Rose Blanche
Livre de Roberto Innocenti et
Christophe Gallaz
publié en mars 1985.
Aquarelle

Art Director · Art Direktor · Directeur Artistique · Anita Turpin

Publisher · Verlag · Editeur · Weidenfeld Publishers Limited

Jesus Mary Delahunty
Jacket for the book by
David MacSweeney
published in the Spring 1985.
Water-colour, gouache and ink

Jesus Mary Delahunty
Umschlag für das Buch von David
MacSweeney
herausgegeben im Frühjahr 1985.
Wasserfarben, Gouache und
Tusche

Jesus Mary Delahunty
Couverture du livre de
David MacSweeney
publié au printemps de 1985.
Aquarelle, gouache et encre

Art Director · Art Direktor · Directeur Artistique · Steve Kent

Publisher · Verlag · Editeur · Penguin Books Limited

Triptych	Triptyk	Triptyque
Jacket illustration for the book	Umschlag-Illustration für das	Illustration de couverture pour
by Joyce Carey	Buch von Joyce Carey	le livre de Joyce Carey
published in May 1985.	herausgegeben im Mai 1985.	publié en mai 1985.
Chalk Pastel	Kreide-Pastell	Pastel de craie

Art Director · Art Direktor · Directeur Artistique · Patrick Mortemore

Designer · Gestalter · Maquettiste · Aruna Mathur

Publisher · Verlag · Editeur · Fontana Books

An Impossible God
Jacket illustration for the book
by Frank Topping
published in March 1985.
Gouache

Ein unmöglicher Gott
Umschlag-Illustration für das
Buch von Frank Topping
herausgegeben im März 1985.
Gouache

Un Dieu impossible
Illustration de couverture du
livre de Frank Topping
publié en mars 1985.
Gouache

Art Director · Art Direktor · Directeur Artistique · John McConnell

Designer · Gestalter · Maquettiste · John Rushworth

Design Group · Design Gruppe · Equipe de Graphistes · Pentagram

Publisher · Verlag · Editeur · Faber & Faber

W. H. Auden Collected	W. H. Auden Gesammelte	Anthologie de Poèmes de
Shorter Poems 1927-1957	kürzere Gedichte 1927-1957	W. H. Auden 1927–1957
Book jacket	Buchumschlag	Couverture de livre
Published in April 1985.	Herausgegeben im April 1985.	Publié en avril 1985.
Gouache	Gouache	Gouache

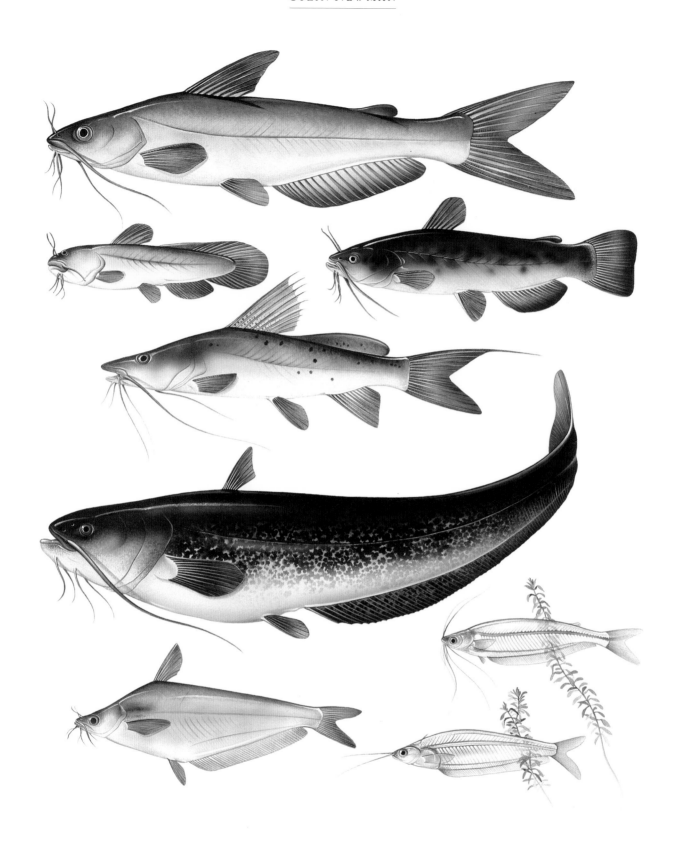

Art Director · Art Direktor · Directeur Artistique · John Bigg

Publisher · Verlag · Editeur · Longman Group Limited

| Catfish of the World From The Longman Illustrated Animal Encyclopedia edited by Jinny Johnson with Alwyne Wheeler, Natural History Consultant, published in April 1984. Water-colour | Seewölfe der Welt Aus dem Longman Illustrierten Tierbuch zusammengestellt von Jinny Johnson mit Alwyne Wheeler, Berater in Naturgeschichte, herausgegeben im April 1984. Wasserfarben | Poissons-chats du Monde De l'Encyclopédie animale illustrée Longman éditée par Jinny Johnson avec Alwyne Wheeler, Conseiller d'Histoire Naturelle, publiée en avril 1984. Aquarelle |

Art Director · Art Direktor · Directeur Artistique · Steve Kent

Publisher · Verlag · Editeur · Penguin Books Limited

Penguin Dictionary of	Das Penguin Buch der	Dictionnaire de Proverbes
Proverbs	Sprichwörter	Penguin
Book jacket	Buchumschlag	Illustration de Couverture
Published in 1984.	Herausgegeben 1984.	publié en 1984.
Acrylics	Acryl	Acryliques

Designer · Gestalter · Maquettiste · Mimmo Cozzolino, David Hughes

Publisher · Verlag · Editeur · Omnibus Press

Eureka. The Songs That Made Australia Published in October 1984. Scraperboard	Eureka. Die Lieder Australiens Herausgegeben im Oktober 1984. Schabtechnik	Eureka. Les Chansons qui ont fait l'Australie Publié en octobre 1984. Carte grattage

Designer · Gestalter · Maquettiste · Mimmo Cozzolino, David Hughes

Publisher · Verlag · Editeur · Omnibus Press

Eureka. The Songs That Made
Australia
Published in October 1984.
Scraperboard

Eureka. Die Lieder Australiens
Herausgegeben im Oktober
1984.
Schabtechnik

Eureka. Les Chansons qui ont
fait l'Australie
publié en octobre 1984.
Carte grattage

Designer · Gestalter · Maquettiste · Simon Loxley

Publisher · Verlag · Editeur · J. M. Dent & Sons Limited

Traitors Purse	Der Schatz der Verräter	Bourse de traitre
Jacket illustration for the book	Umschlag-Illustration für das	Illustration de couverture pour
by Margery Allingham	Buch von Margery Allingham	le livre de Margery Allingham
published in May 1985.	herausgegeben im Mai 1985.	publié en mai 1985.
Gouache	Gouache	Gouache

Art Director · Art Direktor · Directeur Artistique · Denise Brown

Publisher · Verlag · Editeur · Mitchell Beazley Limited

Dreaming	Träumen	Rêvant
Jacket illustration for the book by	Umschlag-Illustration für das	Illustration de couverture pour
Julia and Derek Parker	Buch von Julia und Derek Parker	le livre de Julia et Derek Parker
published in the Autumn 1985.	herausgegeben im Herbst 1985.	publié en automne 1985.
Collage and water-colour	Collage und Wasserfarben	Collage et aquarelle

Art Director · Art Direktor · Directeur Artistique · Aruna Mathur

Publisher · Verlag · Editeur · J. M. Dent & Sons Limited

The Courts of Morning
Jacket illustration for the book
by John Buchan
published in 1984.
Inks

Die Höfe des Morgens
Umschlag-Illustration für das
Buch von John Buchan
herausgegeben 1984.
Tusche

Les Cours du matin
Illustration de couverture pour
le livre de John Buchan
publié en 1984.
Encres

Art Director · Art Direktor · Directeur Artistique · Miles Huddleston

Publisher · Verlag · Editeur · Constable & Company Limited

Broadcasting in Education
Jacket illustration for the book
by Anthony Bates
published in September 1984.
Pen and ink

Sendungen im Schulwesen
Umschlag-Illustration für das
Buch von Anthony Bates
herausgegeben im September
1984.
Feder und Tusche

Radiodiffusion dans
l'enseignement
Illustration de couverture pour
le livre d'Anthony Bates
publié en septembre 1984.
Plume et encre

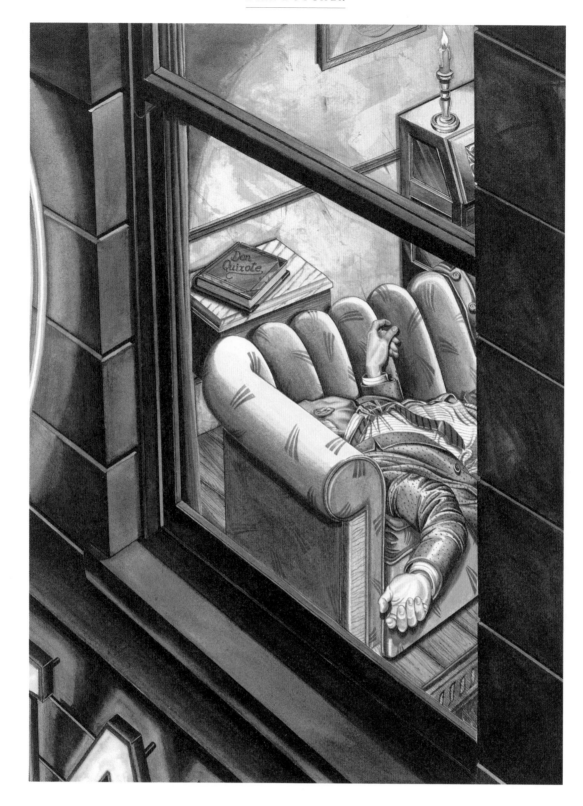

Art Director · Art Direktor · Directeur Artistique · Miles Huddleston

Designer · Gestalter · Maquettiste · Bill Butcher

Publisher · Verlag · Editeur · Constable & Company Limited

Above The Dark Circus
Jacket illustration for the book
by Hugh Walpole
published in April 1985.
Water-colour

Über dem dunklen Zirkus
Umschlag-Illustration für das
Buch von Hugh Walpole
herausgegeben im April 1985.
Wasserfarben

Au-dessus du sombre cirque
Illustration de couverture pour
le livre de Hugh Walpole
publié en avril 1985.
Aquarelle

Art Director · Art Direktor · Directeur Artistique · Miles Huddleston

Designer · Gestalter · Maquettiste · Bill Butcher

Publisher · Verlag · Editeur · Constable & Company Limited

Post Mortem
Jacket illustration for the book
by Guy Cullingford
published in April 1985.
Water-colour

Post Mortem
Umschlag-Illustration für das
Buch von Guy Cullingford
herausgegeben im April 1985.
Wasserfarben

Autopsie
Illustration de couverture pour
le livre de Guy Cullingford
publié en avril 1985.
Aquarelle

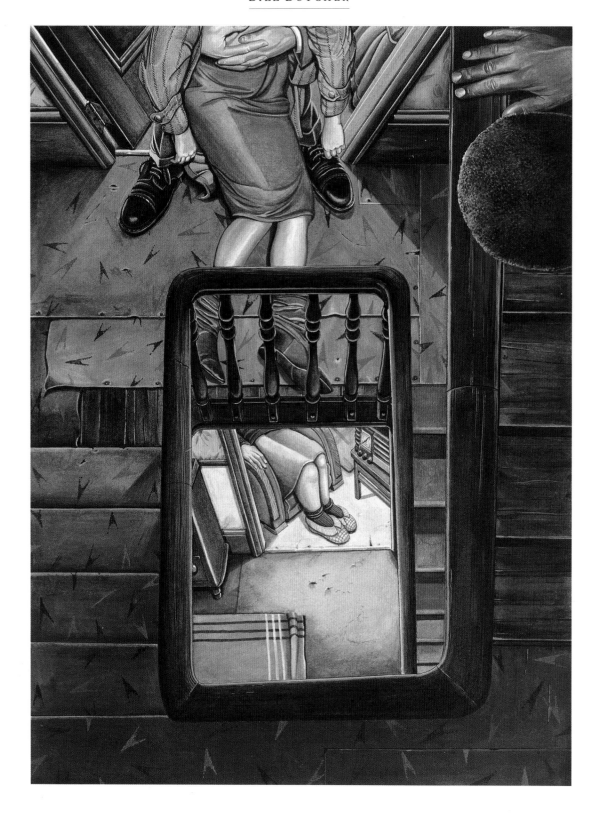

Art Director · Art Direktor · Directeur Artistique · Miles Huddleston

Designer · Gestalter · Maquettiste · Bill Butcher

Publisher · Verlag · Editeur · Constable & Company Limited

A Dark Corner	Eine dunkle Ecke	Un coin sombre
Jacket illustration for the book	Umschlag-Illustration für das	Illustration de couverture pour
by Celia Dale	Buch von Celia Dale	le livre de Celia Dale
published in April 1985.	herausgegeben im April 1985.	publié en avril 1985.
Water-colour	Wasserfarben	Aquarelle

Art Director · Art Direktor · Directeur Artistique · Miles Huddleston

Designer · Gestalter · Maquettiste · Bill Butcher

Publisher · Verlag · Editeur · Constable & Company Limited

Inspector Ghote	Inspektor Ghote auf	L'Inspecteur Ghote
Hunts the Peacock	der Jagd nach dem Pfau	chasse le paon
Jacket illustration for the book	Umschlag-Illustration für das	Illustration de couverture pour
by H. R. F. Keating.	Buch von H. R. F. Keating.	le livre de H. R. F. Keating.
Water-colour	Wasserfarben	Aquarelle

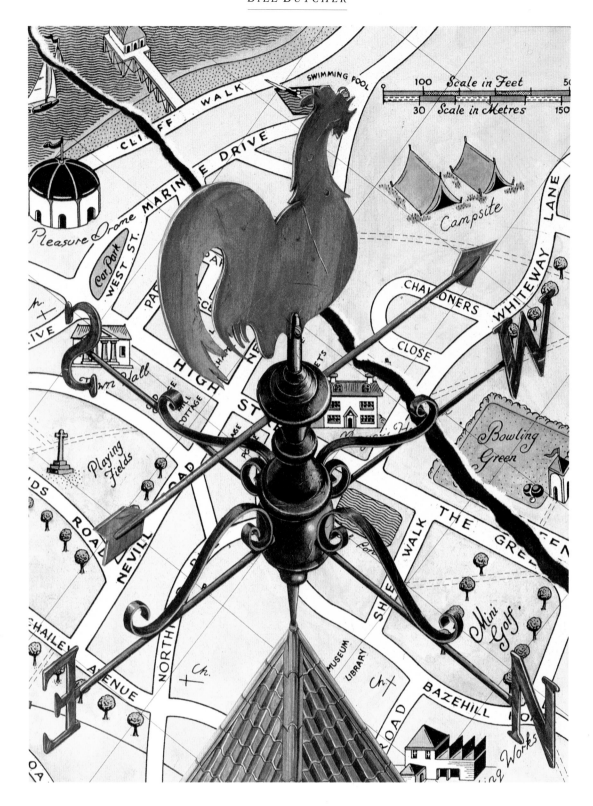

Art Director · Art Direktor · Directeur Artistique · Miles Huddleston

Designer · Gestalter · Maquettiste · Bill Butcher

Publisher · Verlag · Editeur · Constable & Company Limited

The Crack in the Teacup Jacket illustration for the book by Michael Gilbert published in April 1985. Water-colour and Xerox	Der Sprung in der Teetasse Umschlag-Illustration für das Buch von Michael Gilbert herausgegeben im April 1985. Wasserfarben und Fotokopien	La fêlure dans la tasse à thé Illustration de couverture pour le livre de Michael Gilbert publié en avril 1985. Aquarelle et Xerox

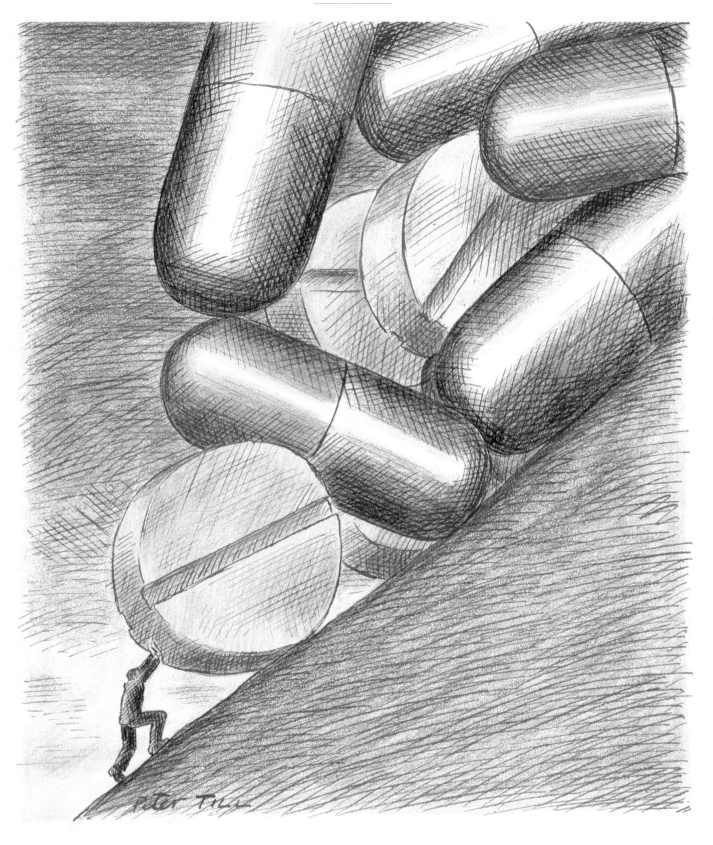

Art Director · Art Direktor · Directeur Artistique · Aruna Mathur

Publisher · Verlag · Editeur · Fontana Books

Roche Versus Adams	Roche gegen Adams	Roche contre Adams
Jacket illustration for the book	Umschlag-Illustration für das	Illustration de couverture pour
by Stanley Adams	Buch von Stanley Adams	le livre de Stanley Adams
published in 1985.	herausgegeben 1985.	publié en 1985.
Pen, ink and coloured pencils	Feder, Tusche und Farbstifte	Plume, encre et crayons de couleur

Art Director · Art Direktor · Directeur Artistique · Ian Hughes

Publisher · Verlag · Editeur · Harrap Limited

Treasure Island	Schatzinsel	L'île au trésor
Illustration from the book by	Illustration aus dem Buch von	Illustration du livre de Robert
Robert Louis Stevenson	Robert Louis Stevenson	Louis Stevenson
Published October 1985.	herausgegeben im Oktober 1985.	publié en octobre 1985.
Inks	Tusche	Encres

Art Director · Art Direktor · Directeur Artistique · Mike Hannett

Copywriter · Texter · Rédacteur · Dave Buchanan

Advertising Agency · Werbeagentur · Agence de Publicité · T.B.W.A.

Client · Auftraggeber · Client · Dunlopillo Division (UK)

An Unsettled Night Brings	Eine unruhige Nacht bringt	Une nuit agitée amène une
A Gloomy Day	einen verdrießlichen Tag	journée lugubre
Consumer advertisement	Verbraucherwerbung	Publicité de consommation
for beds.	für Betten.	pour les lits.
Gouache	Gouache	Gouache

Art Director · Art Direktor · Directeur Artistique · Mike Hannett

Copywriter · Texter · Rédacteur · Dave Buchanan

Advertising Agency · Werbeagentur · Agence de Publicité · T.B.W.A.

Client · Auftraggeber · Client · Dunlopillo Division (UK)

A Poor Night's Sleep Can Turn
Your Whole Day Into
A Nightmare
Consumer advertisement
for beds.
Gouache

Durch eine schlaflose Nacht
kann Ihr ganzer Tag ein
Alptraum werden
Verbraucherwerbung
für Betten.
Gouache

Mal dormir peut transformer
votre journée en cauchemar
Publicité de consommation
pour les lits.
Gouache

Art Director · Art Direktor · Directeur Artistique · Hansjoachim Dietrich

Copywriter · Texter · Rédacteur · Helga Falkenstein

Advertising Agency · Werbeagentur · Agence de Publicité · DF&H Werbeagentur GmbH

Client · Auftraggeber · Client · Sopexa/BNICE

Just What Sort Of Trees Are These That Keep Normans Hopping? Advertising campaign for Calvados. Ink in black and white	Was sind das bloss für Bäume, die den Normannen Beine machen? Werbekampagne für Calvados. Tusche in schwarz-weiß	Quels sont donc ces arbres qui donnent du ressort aux Normands? Campagne publicitaire pour le Calvados. Encre en noir et blanc

Art Director · Art Direktor · Directeur Artistique · Hansjoachim Dietrich

Copywriter · Texter · Rédacteur · Helga Falkenstein

Advertising Agency · Werbeagentur · Agence de Publicité · DF&H Werbeagentur GmbH

Client · Auftraggeber · Client · Sopexa/BNICE

What Are Normans Dreaming Of When They Are Drinking Calvados? Advertising campaign for Calvados. Black and white plus coloured Ink and oil pastels	Wovon träumen die Normannen, wenn Sie Calvados trinken? Werbekampagne für Calvados. Schwarz-weiße und Farbige Tusche und Ölpastellfarben	A quoi rêvent les Normands lorsqui'ils boivent du Calvados? Campagne publicitaire pour le Calvados. Noir et blanc plus Encre de couleur et pastels à l'huile

Art Director · Art Direktor · Directeur Artistique · Hansjoachim Dietrich

Copywriter · Texter · Rédacteur · Helga Falkenstein

Advertising Agency · Werbeagentur · Agence de Publicité · DF&H Werbeagentur GmbH

Client · Auftraggeber · Client · Sopexa/BNICE

Is It All Those Sterling Apples, The Poultry Or The Normans After All? Advertising campaign for Calvados. Black and white plus coloured Ink and oil pastels	Liegt es nun an den vielen guten Äpfeln, an den Hühnern oder doch an den Normannen? Werbekampagne für Calvados. Schwarz-weiße und Farbige Tusche und Ölpastellfarben	S'agit-il de toutes ces bonnes pommes, des poules ou tout simplement des Normands? Campagne publicitaire pour le Calvados. Noir et blanc plus Encre de couleur et pastels à l'huile

Art Director · Art Direktor · Directeur Artistique · Hansjoachim Dietrich

Copywriter · Texter · Rédacteur · Helga Falkenstein

Advertising Agency · Werbeagentur · Agence de Publicité · DF&H Werbeagentur GmbH

Client · Auftraggeber · Client · Sopexa/BNICE

What Do You Call That Breed
Of Frenchmen Again, The
Ones Who Are So Bananas
About Apples?
Advertising campaign
for Calvados.
Black and white plus coloured
Ink and oil pastels

Wie heisst noch gleich diese
Art von Franzosen, die so
unglaublich auf Äpfeln steht?
Werbekampagne für Calvados.
Schwarz-weiße und Farbige
Tusche und Ölpastellfarben

Comment appelle-t-on déjà ce
genre de Français, ceux qui
sont si friands de pommes?
Campagne publicitaire pour
le Calvados.
Noir et blanc plus Encre de
couleur et pastels à l'huile

Art Director · Art Direktor · Directeur Artistique · Tom Moult

Copywriter · Texter · Rédacteur · Simon Collins

Advertising Agency · Werbeagentur · Agence de Publicité · J. Walter Thompson Company Limited

Client · Auftraggeber · Client · John Harvey and Sons

Symmering in Hot Water Tubecard illustration for Cockburns Special Reserve Port. Pen and ink and water-colour	Symmering in heißen Wassern Illustration zur Werbung auf der U-Bahn für Cockburns Special Reserve Portwein. Feder und Tusche und Wasserfarben	Symmering échaudé Illustration pour affichette de métro pour le porto Cockburns Special Reserve. Plume et encre et aquarelle

Art Director · Art Direktor · Directeur Artistique · Tom Moult

Copywriter · Texter · Rédacteur · Simon Collins

Advertising Agency · Werbeagentur · Agence de Publicité · J. Walter Thompson Company Limited

Client · Auftraggeber · Client · John Harvey and Sons

Miles Out of Port	Miles ohne Portwein	Loin du port et sans porto
Tubecard illustration	Illustration zur Werbung	Illustration pour affichette
for Cockburns Special	auf der U-Bahn	de métro
Reserve Port.	für Cockburns Special	pour le porto Cockburns
Pen and ink and water-colour	Reserve Portwein.	Special Reserve.
	Feder und Tusche und	Plume et encre et aquarelle
	Wasserfarben	

Art Director · Art Direktor · Directeur Artistique · Vicki Miller and Andy Vargo

Copywriter · Texter · Rédacteur · Vicki Miller and Andy Vargo

Client · Auftraggeber · Client · Norwich School of Art

Leaping Salmon	Springender Lachs	Saumon bondissant.
Poster.	Plakat.	Affiche.
Gouache and ink	Gouache und Tusche	Gouache et encre

Art Director · Art Direktor · Directeur Artistique · Bob Gill		
Copywriter · Texter · Rédacteur · Peter Cayless		
Advertising Agency · Werbeagentur · Agence de Publicité · Foote Cone & Belding		
Client · Auftraggeber · Client · Gordons Gin		

It's Got To Be Gordons	Es muß einfach Gordons sein	Il faut que ce soit du Gordons
Consumer advertisement for	Verbraucherwerbung für	Publicité de consommation
Gordon's White Lady.	Gordons White Lady.	pour
Coloured pencils	Farbstifte	Gordon's White Lady.
		Crayons de couleur

Art Director · Art Direktor · Directeur Artistique · David Holmes

Copywriter · Texter · Rédacteur · Nick Salaman

Advertising Agency · Werbeagentur · Agence de Publicité · Holmes Knight Ritchie Limited

Client · Auftraggeber · Client · Macallan

It Sleeps Alone	Es schläft allein	Il dort seul
Press advertisement for	Pressewerbung für	Publicité de presse pour le
Malt Whisky.	Malz-Whisky.	Whisky au malt.
Pen and ink in black and white	Feder und Tusche in schwarz-weiß	Plume et encre en noir et blanc

Art Director · Art Direktor · Directeur Artistique · Mary Roberts

Copywriter · Texter · Rédacteur · Neil Bevan

Advertising Agency · Werbeagentur · Agence de Publicité · Holmes Knight Ritchie Limited

Client · Auftraggeber · Client · Cosmopolitan

Better Chaste Than Chased?
Press advertisement for an
article on
feminine celibacy.
Pen and ink in black and white

Lieber keusch als verfolgt?
Pressewerbung für einen
Artikel über
weibliches Zölibat.
Feder und Tusche in
schwarz-weiß

Mieux vaut être chaste que
chassée?
Publicité de presse pour un
article sur
le célibat féminin.
Plume et encre en noir et blanc

Art Director · Art Direktor · Directeur Artistique · Jeremy Pemberton

Copywriter · Texter · Rédacteur · Alan Page

Advertising Agency · Werbeagentur · Agence de Publicité · Yellowhammer

Client · Auftraggeber · Client · Marley Extrusions Limited

If We Simply Kept To British Standards An Unexpected Downfall Could Be Our Downfall Too Consumer advertisement for the Plastics Industry. Pastels	Wenn wir uns nur an britische Standardwerte halten würden, könnte ein unverhoffter Regenfall auch unseren Untergang bedeuten Verbraucherwerbung für die Plastik-Industrie. Pastellfarben	Si nous nous en tenions aux normes britanniques un écroulement inattendu pourrait aussi être notre écroulement Publicité de consommation pour l'industrie des plastiques. Pastels

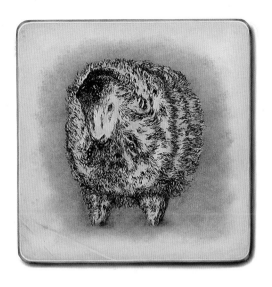

Art Director · Art Direktor · Directeur Artistique · Kit Marr

Copywriter · Texter · Rédacteur · Neil Fazakerley

Advertising Agency · Werbeagentur · Agence de Publicité · Davidson Pearce

Client · Auftraggeber · Client · International Wool Secretariat

Beware of the Wolf in Sheep's Clothing	Hüten Sie sich vor dem Wolf im Schafspelz	Prenez garde du loup déguisé en brebis
Consumer advertisement for woollen menswear.	Verbraucherwerbung für Wollsachen für Männer.	Publicité de consommation pour les vêtements d'homme en laine.
Water-colour, pencil and gouache	Wasserfarben, Bleistift und Gouache	Aquarelle, crayon et gouache

Art Director · Art Direktor · Directeur Artistique · Kit Marr

Copywriter · Texter · Rédacteur · Neil Fazakerley

Advertising Agency · Werbeagentur · Agence de Publicité · Davidson Pearce

Client · Auftraggeber · Client · International Wool Secretariat

Beware of the Wolf in Sheep's Clothing Consumer advertisement for woollen menswear. Ink and scraperboard in black and white	Hüten Sie sich vor dem Wolf im Schafspelz Verbraucherwerbung für Wollsachen für Männer. Tusche und Schabtechnik in schwarz-weiß	Prenez garde du loup déguisé en brebis Publicité de consommation pour les vêtements d'homme en laine. Encre et carte grattage en noir et blanc

Art Director · Art Direktor · Directeur Artistique · Kit Marr

Copywriter · Texter · Rédacteur · Neil Fazakerley

Advertising Agency · Werbeagentur · Agence de Publicité · Davidson Pearce

Client · Auftraggeber · Client · International Wool Secretariat

Beware of the Wolf in Sheep's Clothing Consumer advertisement for woollen menswear. Water-colour, ink and gouache	Hüten Sie sich vor dem Wolf im Schafspelz Verbraucherwerbung für Wollsachen für Männer. Wasserfarben, Tusche und Gouache	Prenez garde du loup déguisé en brebis Publicité de consommation pour les vêtements d'homme en laine. Aquarelle, encre et gouache

GLC MUSIC IN THE OPEN AIR
KENWOOD LAKESIDE 8.oopm EVERY SATURDAY UNTIL 11th AUGUST.

SUMMER
1984
GLC WORKING FOR LONDON

Art Director · Art Direktor · Directeur Artistique · Joanna Wenley

Advertising Agency · Werbeagentur · Agence de Publicité · Boase Massimi Pollitt Univas Partnership Limited

Client · Auftraggeber · Client · Greater London Council

GLC Music in the Open Air	GLC Musik im Freien	Musique en plein air du GLC
Poster for London Transport	Plakat für London Transport	Affiche de publicité sur les bus
buses advertising	Busse zur Werbung	de London Transport
concerts at Kenwood.	von Konzerten in Kenwood.	pour les concerts à Kenwood.
Coloured pencils	Farbstifte	Crayons de couleur

Art Director · Art Direktor · Directeur Artistique · Joanna Wenley

Copywriter · Texter · Rédacteur · Tim Riley

Advertising Agency · Werbeagentur · Agence de Publicité · Boase Massimi Pollitt Univas Partnership Limited

Client · Auftraggeber · Client · Greater London Council

GLC Thamesday	GLC Tag der Themse	GLC Journée de la Tamise
Cross-track poster site on the	Plakat eingesetzt auf U-Bahn	Site de publicité en diagonale
underground for a	Stationen für ein	dans le métro pour une
summer season festival.	sommerliches Fest.	saison de festival d'été.
Water-colour	Wasserfarben	Aquarelle

Art Director · Art Direktor · Directeur Artistique · John Jolly

Copywriter · Texter · Rédacteur · Barry Wrightson

Advertising Agency · Werbeagentur · Agence de Publicité · D'Arcy-MacManus & Masius

Client · Auftraggeber · Client · Ind Coope Burton Brewery

When You've Earned a Great Pint Go For a Burton 48 sheet poster illustrating the Industrial Revolution. Oil on canvas	Wenn Sie ein gutes Bier verdient haben verlangen Sie ein Burtons 48-Blatt Plakat zur Illustration der industriellen Revolution. Öl auf Leinwand	Quand vous avez mérité une bonne pinte Demandez une bière de Burton Affiche en 48 feuilles illustrant la revolution industrielle. Huile sur toile

Art Director · Art Direktor · Directeur Artistique · David Christensen

Copywriter · Texter · Rédacteur · Alfredo Marcantonio

Advertising Agency · Werbeagentur · Agence de Publicité · Lowe Howard-Spink Campbell-Ewald

Client · Auftraggeber · Client · Long John International Limited

The Long Boat International press advertisement for Long John Whiskey. Acrylics	Das Grossboot Internationale Pressewerbung für Long John Whiskey. Acryl	Le Bateau Long Publicité de presse internationale pour le Whiskey Long John. Acryliques

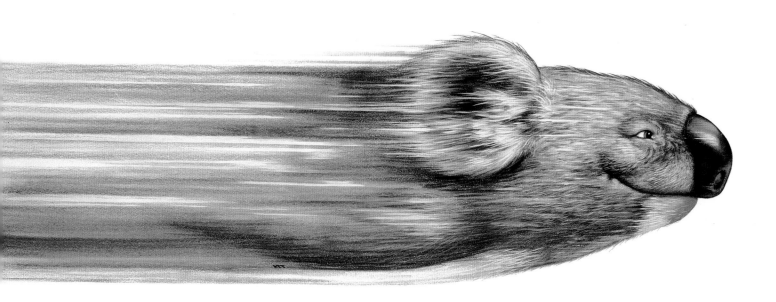

Art Director · Art Direktor · Directeur Artistique · Mick Devito-French

Copywriter · Texter · Rédacteur · Derek Day

Advertising Agency · Werbeagentur · Agence de Publicité · Wight Collins Rutherford Scott

Client · Auftraggeber · Client · Qantas Airlines

Fastest to Sydney Poster advertising Qantas Airlines. Gouache and pastels	Schnellste Verbindung nach Sydney Plakatwerbung für Qantas Airlines. Gouache und Pastellfarben	Le plus rapide pour Sydney Affiche de publicité pour Qantas Airlines. Gouache et pastels

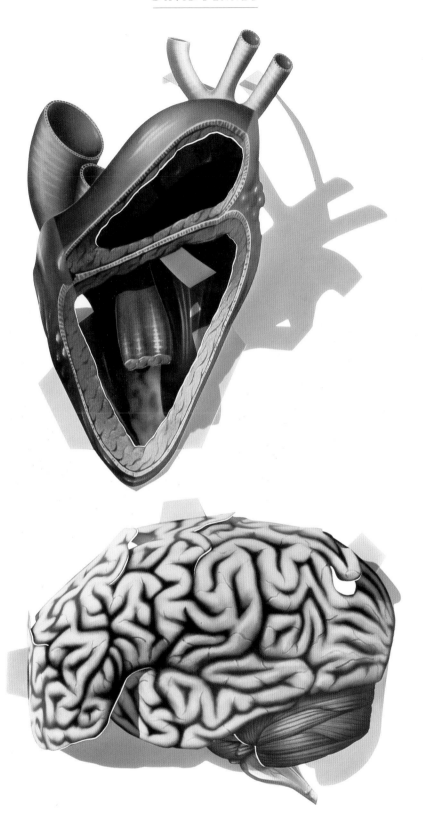

Art Director · Art Direktor · Directeur Artistique · Malcolm Gaskin

Copywriter · Texter · Rédacteur · Neil Patterson

Advertising Agency · Werbeagentur · Agence de Publicité · T.B.W.A.

Client · Auftraggeber · Client · Central Office of Information

What Part of Your Anatomy
makes You Want to become a
Nurse?
Consumer advertisement for
nursing recruitment.
Cardboard engineering and
water-colour

Welcher Teil Ihrer Anatomie
verleitet Sie dazu,
Krankenschwester zu werden?
Verbraucherwerbung zur
Anwerbung von
Krankenschwestern.
Karton-Konstruktion und
Wasserfarben

Quelle partie de votre anatomie
vous pousse à vouloir devenir
infirmière?
Publicité de consommation
pour le recrutement des
infirmiers.
Assemblage de carton et
aquarelle

Art Director · Art Direktor · Directeur Artistique · Alan Waldie

Copywriter · Texter · Rédacteur · Adrian Holmes

Advertising Agency · Werbeagentur · Agence de Publicité · Lowe Howard-Spink Campbell-Ewald

Client · Auftraggeber · Client · Long John International Limited

Plymouth Gin is not the only way to tell a Gentleman Press advertisement. Line illustrations and water-colour wash	Plymouth Gin ist nicht der einzige Weg, einen wahren Gentleman zu erkennen Pressewerbung. Strichillustrationen und Wasserfarben laviert	Ce n'est pas uniquement par le Plymouth gin qu'on reconnaît un gentleman Publicité de presse. Illustrations linéaires et lavis d'aquarelle

Art Director · Art Direktor · Directeur Artistique · John Dodson

Copywriter · Texter · Rédacteur · Peter Neeves

Advertising Agency · Werbeagentur · Agence de Publicité · Doyle Dane Bernbach Limited

Design Group · Design Gruppe · Equipe de Graphistes · Wolff Olins

Client · Auftraggeber · Client · 3i (Investors in Industry plc)

Sometimes you need a Fund of Imagination as well as Funds Press advertisement for finance and financial services. Ink and water-colour

Manchmal brauchen Sie eine Fülle von Einfällen ebensosehr wie Geldmittel Pressewerbung für Finanzen und Finanzdienste. Tusche und Wasserfarben

Il vous faut quelquefois un fonds d'imagination en plus des fonds Publicité de presse pour financement et services financiers. Encre et aquarelle

Art Director · Kunstredakteur · Redacteur Artistique · Lynn Trickett and Brian Webb

Designer · Gestalter · Maquettiste · Tony Hansle

Design Group · Design Gruppe · Equipe de Graphistes · Trickett & Webb Limited

Publisher · Verlag · Editeur · Augustus Martin/Trickett & Webb Limited

The Boss – January	Der Chef – Januar	Le patron – janvier
The Office Calendar.	Der Büro-Kalender.	Le calendrier du bureau.
Screenprinting	Siebdruck	Sérigraphie

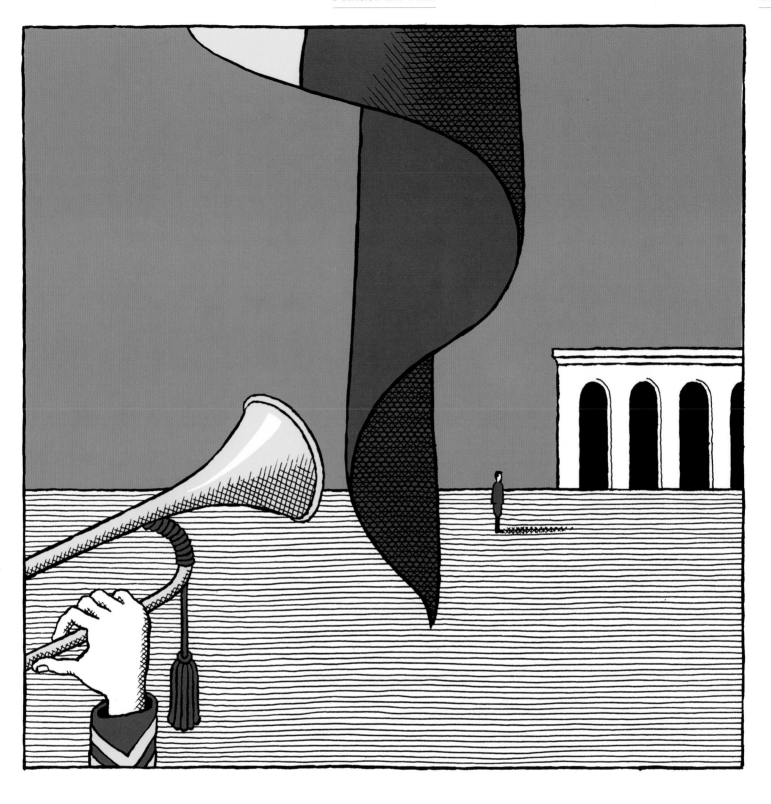

Art Director · Kunstredakteur · Redacteur Artistique · Lynn Trickett and Brian Webb

Designer · Gestalter · Maquettiste · Tony Hansle

Design Group · Design Gruppe · Equipe de Graphistes · Trickett & Webb Limited

Publisher · Verlag · Editeur · Augustus Martin/Trickett & Webb Limited

Last Post – February	Letzte Postsammlung –	Dernière levée – février
The Office Calendar.	Februar	Le calendrier du bureau.
Screenprinting	Der Büro-Kalender.	Sérigraphie
	Siebdruck	

Art Director · Kunstredakteur · Redacteur Artistique · Lynn Trickett and Brian Webb

Designer · Gestalter · Maquettiste · Tony Hansle

Design Group · Design Gruppe · Equipe de Graphistes · Trickett & Webb Limited

Publisher · Verlag · Editeur · Augustus Martin/Trickett & Webb Limited

Tea Break – June	Teepause – Juni	Pause thé – juin
The Office Calendar.	Der Büro-Kalender.	Le calendrier du bureau.
Screenprinting	Siebdruck	Sérigraphie

Art Director · Kunstredakteur · Redacteur Artistique · Lynn Trickett and Brian Webb

Designer · Gestalter · Maquettiste · Tony Hansle

Design Group · Design Gruppe · Equipe de Graphistes · Trickett & Webb Limited

Publisher · Verlag · Editeur · Augustus Martin/Trickett & Webb Limited

Expense Account – November
The Office Calendar.
Screenprinting

Spesenrechnung – November
Der Büro-Kalender.
Siebdruck

Frais de représentation –
novembre
Le calendrier du bureau.
Sérigraphie

Art Director · Kunstredakteur · Redacteur Artistique · Lynn Trickett and Brian Webb

Designer · Gestalter · Maquettiste · Tony Hansle

Design Group · Design Gruppe · Equipe de Graphistes · Trickett & Webb Limited

Publisher · Verlag · Editeur · Augustus Martin/Trickett & Webb Limited

Working Hours – July	Arbeitsstunden – Juli	Heures de travail – juillet
The Office Calendar.	Der Büro-Kalender.	Le calendrier du bureau.
Screenprinting	Siebdruck	Sérigraphie

Art Director · Kunstredakteur · Redacteur Artistique · Lynn Trickett and Brian Webb

Designer · Gestalter · Maquettiste · Tony Hansle

Design Group · Design Gruppe · Equipe de Graphistes · Trickett & Webb Limited

Publisher · Verlag · Editeur · Augustus Martin/Trickett & Webb Limited

Pencil Sharpener – March	Bleistiftspitzer – März	Taille-crayon – mars
The Office Calendar.	Der Büro-Kalender.	Le calendrier du bureau.
Screenprinting	Siebdruck	Sérigraphie

Art Director · Kunstredakteur · Redacteur Artistique · Lynn Trickett and Brian Webb

Designer · Gestalter · Maquettiste · Tony Hansle

Design Group · Design Gruppe · Equipe de Graphistes · Trickett & Webb Limited

Publisher · Verlag · Editeur · Augustus Martin/Trickett & Webb Limited

Red Tape – October	Bürokratismus – Oktober	Paperasserie – octobre
The Office Calendar.	Der Büro-Kalender.	Le calendrier du bureau.
Screenprinting	Siebdruck	Sérigraphie

Art Director · Kunstredakteur · Redacteur Artistique · Lynn Trickett and Brian Webb
Designer · Gestalter · Maquettiste · Tony Hansle
Design Group · Design Gruppe · Equipe de Graphistes · Trickett & Webb Limited
Publisher · Verlag · Editeur · Augustus Martin/Trickett & Webb Limited

The Office Dragon – May	Der Büro-Drachen – Mai	Le dragon du bureau – mai
The Office Calendar.	Der Büro-Kalender.	Le calendrier du bureau.
Screenprinting	Siebdruck	Sérigraphie

Art Director · Kunstredakteur · Redacteur Artistique · Lynn Trickett and Brian Webb

Designer · Gestalter · Maquettiste · Tony Hansle

Design Group · Design Gruppe · Equipe de Graphistes · Trickett & Webb Limited

Publisher · Verlag · Editeur · Augustus Martin/Trickett & Webb Limited

Typing Pool – September	Schreibdienst – September	Le pool dactylo – septembre
The Office Calendar.	Der Büro-Kalender.	Le calendrier du bureau.
Screenprinting	Siebdruck	Sérigraphie

Art Director · Kunstredakteur · Redacteur Artistique · Lynn Trickett and Brian Webb ·

Designer · Gestalter · Maquettiste · Tony Hansle

Design Group · Design Gruppe · Equipe de Graphistes · Trickett & Webb Limited

Publisher · Verlag · Editeur · Augustus Martin/Trickett & Webb Limited

Christmas Party – December
The Office Calendar.
Screenprinting

Weihnachtsparty – Dezember
Der Büro-Kalender.
Siebdruck

Fête de Noël – décembre
Le calendrier du bureau.
Sérigraphie

Art Director · Kunstredakteur · Redacteur Artistique · Lynn Trickett and Brian Webb

Designer · Gestalter · Maquettiste · Tony Hansle

Design Group · Design Gruppe · Equipe de Graphistes · Trickett & Webb Limited

Publisher · Verlag · Editeur · Augustus Martin/Trickett & Webb Limited

Letterhead – April	Briefkopf – April	En-tête – avril
The Office Calendar.	Der Büro-Kalender.	Le calendrier du bureau.
Screenprinting	Siebdruck	Sérigraphie

Art Director · Kunstredakteur · Redacteur Artistique · Lynn Trickett and Brian Webb

Designer · Gestalter · Maquettiste · Tony Hansle

Design Group · Design Gruppe · Equipe de Graphistes · Trickett & Webb Limited

Publisher · Verlag · Editeur · Augustus Martin/Trickett & Webb Limited

Rubber Stamp – August	Gummistempel – August	Tampon – août
The Office Calendar.	Der Büro-Kalender.	Le calendrier du bureau.
Screenprinting	Siebdruck	Sérigraphie

Art Director · Kunstredakteur · Redacteur Artistique · Linda Sutton

Designer · Gestalter · Maquettiste · Roger Cooper

Design Group · Design Gruppe · Equipe de Graphistes · Sutton Cooper

Client · Auftraggeber · Client · Fakes

Car Companion – January	Mitfahrer – Januar	Compagnon de voyage –
Fakes Calendar.	Fakes Kalender.	janvier
Collage and mixed media	Collage und Mischtechnik	Calendrier Fakes.
		Collage et moyens divers

Designer · Gestalter · Maquettiste · Roger Cooper

Design Group · Design Gruppe · Equipe de Graphistes · Sutton Cooper

Client · Auftraggeber · Client · Fakes

But is it Art? – June	Aber ist es Kunst? – Juni	Mais est-ce l'art? – juin
Fakes Calendar.	Fakes Kalender.	Calendrier Fakes.
Collage and mixed media	Collage und Mischtechnik	Collage et moyens divers

Art Director · Kunstredakteur · Redacteur Artistique · Linda Sutton

Designer · Gestalter · Maquettiste · Roger Cooper

Design Group · Design Gruppe · Equipe de Graphistes · Sutton Cooper

Client · Auftraggeber · Client · Fakes

The Scrapbook of Dr. Hoffman — May	Das Sammelbuch des Dr. Hoffman – Mai	L'album du Dr. Hoffman – mai
Fakes Calendar.	Fakes Kalender.	Calendrier Fakes.
Collage and mixed media	Collage und Mischtechnik	Collage et moyens divers

Art Director · Kunstredakteur · Redacteur Artistique · Linda Sutton

Designer · Gestalter · Maquettiste · Roger Cooper

Design Group · Design Gruppe · Equipe de Graphistes · Sutton Cooper

Client · Auftraggeber · Client · Fakes

Ecce Travertine Vinyl –
February
Fakes Calendar.
Gouache

Ecce Travertine Vinyl –
Februar
Fakes Kalender.
Gouache

Vinyle Ecce Travertine –
février
Calendrier Fakes.
Gouache

Art Director · Kunstredakteur · Redacteur Artistique · Linda Sutton

Designer · Gestalter · Maquettiste · Roger Cooper

Design Group · Design Gruppe · Equipe de Graphistes · Sutton Cooper

Client · Auftraggeber · Client · Fakes

Decoy Duck – October	Entenfalle – Oktober	Appeau – octobre
Fakes Calendar.	Fakes Kalender.	Calendrier Fakes.
Ink on Kodatrace	Tusche auf Kodatrace	Encre sur papier Kodatrace

Art Director · Kunstredakteur · Redacteur Artistique · Linda Sutton

Designer · Gestalter · Maquettiste · Roger Cooper

Design Group · Design Gruppe · Equipe de Graphistes · Sutton Cooper

Publisher · Verlag · Editeur · Fakes

Fishing Flies – July	Angelfliegen – Juli	Mouches de pêche – juillet
Fakes Calendar.	Fakes Kalender.	Calendrier Fakes.
Water-colour	Wasserfarben	Aquarelle

Art Director · Kunstredakteur · Redacteur Artistique · Linda Sutton

Designer · Gestalter · Maquettiste · Roger Cooper

Design Group · Design Gruppe · Equipe de Graphistes · Sutton Cooper

Publisher · Verlag · Editeur · Fakes

Which Came First? – March	Was kam zuerst? – März	Quel était le premier? – mars
Fakes Calendar.	Fakes Kalender.	Calendrier Fakes.
Mixed Media	Mischtechnik	Moyens divers

Art Director · Kunstredakteur · Redacteur Artistique · Frank Sully

Design Group · Design Gruppe · Equipe de Graphistes · Perception Design

Gold
Promotional design for a plate.
Lino cut in three colours

Gold
Promotionelle Gestaltung
eines Tellers
Linolschnitt in drei Farben

Or
Design de promotion pour
une assiette.
Gravure sur lino en
trois couleurs

Designer · Gestalter · Maquettiste · Peter Windett

Design Group · Design Gruppe · Equipe de Graphistes · Peter Windett & Associates

Client · Auftraggeber · Client · Crabtree & Evelyn

| Labels for Tartare Sauce. | Etiketten für Tartare Soße. | Etiquettes pour sauce tartare. |
| Water-colour | Wasserfarben | Aquarelle |

Designer · Gestalter · Maquettiste · Peter Windett

Design Group · Design Gruppe · Equipe de Graphistes · Peter Windett & Associates

Client · Auftraggeber · Client · Crabtree & Evelyn

Labels for Mayonnaise.	Etiketten für Mayonnaise.	Etiquettes pour Mayonnaise.
Water-colour	Wasserfarben	Aquarelle

Designer · Gestalter · Maquettiste · Peter Windett

Design Group · Design Gruppe · Equipe de Graphistes · Peter Windett & Associates

Client · Auftraggeber · Client · Crabtree & Evelyn

Labels for Horseradish Sauce. Water-colour	Etiketten für Meerettichsoße. Wasserfarben	Etiquettes pour sauce de raifort. Aquarelle

Art Director · Kunstredakteur · Redacteur Artistique · Lynn Trickett and Brian Webb

Designer · Gestalter · Maquettiste · Ian Cockburn

Design Group · Design Gruppe · Equipe de Graphistes · Trickett & Webb Limited

Client · Auftraggeber · Client · British Telecom Corporate Services

Graduate Biographies	Biografien von Graduierten	Biographies de diplômés
Recruitment brochure.	Broschüre zur	Brochure de recrutement.
Gouache	Personalwerbung.	Gouache
	Gouache	

SEVENTEEN · PENCE
WATER · MUSIC
George Frideric Handel

THIRTY · ONE · PENCE
THE · FIRST · CUCKOO
Frederick Delius

TWENTY · TWO · PENCE
THE · PLANETS · SUITE
Gustav Holst

THIRTY · FOUR · PENCE
SEA · PICTURES
Edward Elgar

Art Director · Kunstredakteur · Redacteur Artistique · Barry Robinson

Client · Auftraggeber · Client · The Post Office

Handel (a) Holst (b)	Händel (a) Holst (b)	Handel (a) Holst (b)
Delius (c) Elgar (d)	Delius (c) Elgar (d)	Delius (c) Elgar (d)
Royal Mail Postage Stamps.	Royal Mail Briefmarken.	Timbres poste.
Oils	Öl	Huiles

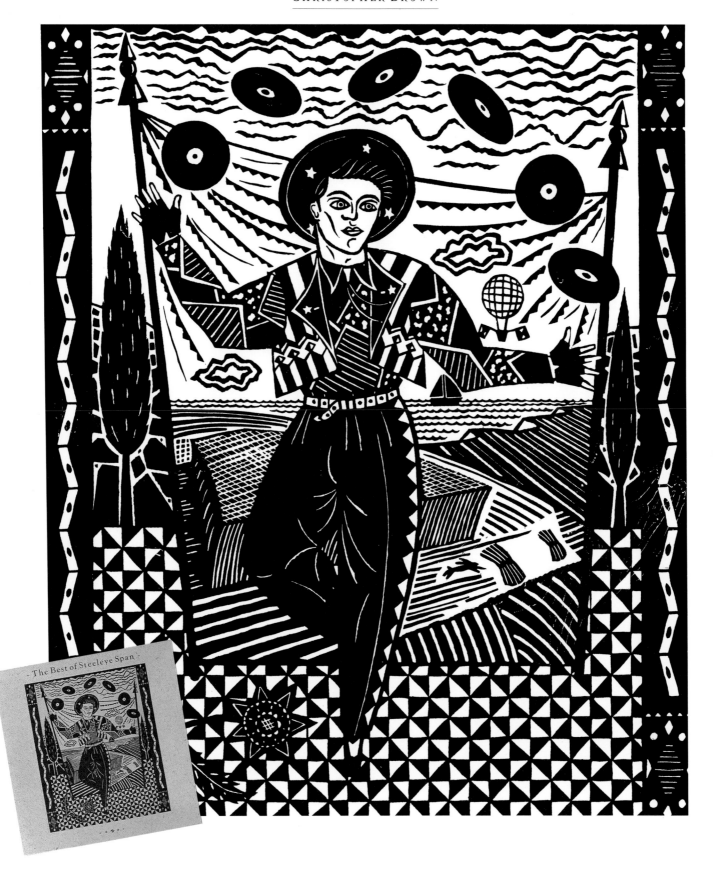

Designer · Gestalter · Maquettiste · John Pashe

Client · Auftraggeber · Client · Chrysalis Records

The Best of Steeleye Span	Das Beste von Steeleye Span	Le meilleur de Steeleye Span
Record Cover.	Plattenhülle.	Enveloppe de disque.
Lino cut	Linolschnitt	Gravure sur lino

Designer · Gestalter · Maquettiste · John Gorham

Client · Auftraggeber · Client · Character Photosetting

Christmas Card.	Weihnachtskarte.	Carte de Noël.
Wood-engraving in black and white	Holzschnitt in schwarz-weiß	Gravure sur bois en noir et blanc

Art Director · Kunstredakteur · Redacteur Artistique · Aziz Cami

Designer · Gestalter · Maquettiste · Steve Gibbons

Design Group · Design Gruppe · Equipe de Graphistes · The Partners

Client · Auftraggeber · Client · St. James's Club

Christmas Card.
Scraperboard in black
and white

Weihnachtskarte.
Schabtechnik in schwarz-weiß

Carte de Noël.
Carte grattage en noir et blanc

Art Director · Kunstredakteur · Redacteur Artistique · Robert Fairman

Designer · Gestalter · Maquettiste · Brian Grimwood

Design Group · Design Gruppe · Equipe de Graphistes · Creative Results Limited

Client · Auftraggeber · Client · Sony UK Limited

Boy George, King of Spades
For a promotional pack
of cards.
Gouache and crayon

Boy George, Pik-König
Für einen promotionellen
Satz Spielkarten.
Gouache und Farbstifte

Boy George, Roi de Pique
Pour un jeu de cartes de
promotion.
Gouache et pastel

Art Director · Kunstredakteur · Redacteur Artistique · Howard Milton

Designer · Gestalter · Maquettiste · Brian Grimwood and Howard Milton

Design Group · Design Gruppe · Equipe de Graphistes · Smith & Milton

Client · Auftraggeber · Client · J. A. Sharwood & Company Limited

Sharwoods Packaging.
Gouache

Verpackung für Sharwoods.
Gouache

Emballage Sharwoods.
Gouache

Art Director · Kunstredakteur · Redacteur Artistique · Bruno Tilley

Designer · Gestalter · Maquettiste · Bruno Tilley and Stephanie Nash

Client · Auftraggeber · Client · Island Records

Design for Reggae Greats Series.	Design für die Serie Reggae-Größen.	Design pour Série Reggae célèbres.
Cut out paper	Geschnittenes Papier	Découpage

Art Director · Kunstredakteur · Redacteur Artistique · Bruno Tilley

Designer · Gestalter · Maquettiste · Bruno Tilley and Stephanie Nash

Client · Auftraggeber · Client · Island Records

Strictly for Rockers	Ausschließlich für Rocker	Strictement pour Rockers
Record Cover.	Plattenhülle.	Enveloppe de disque.
Cut out paper	Geschnittenes Papier	Découpage

Art Director · Kunstredakteur · Rédacteur Artistique · Siobahn Keaney

Designer · Gestalter · Maquettiste · Bush Hollyhead

Design Group · Design Gruppe · Equipe de Graphistes · David Davies Associates

Client · Auftraggeber · Client · Midland Bank

Making the Right Connections Brochure for Midland Bank. Water-colour and crayon	Die richtigen Beziehungen schaffen Broschüre für die Midland Bank. Wasserfarben und Farbstifte	Etablir de bonnes relations Brochure pour la Midland Bank. Aquarelle et pastel

Art Director · Kunstredakteur · Redacteur Artistique · David Hillman

Designer · Gestalter · Maquettiste · Bush Hollyhead

Design Group · Design Gruppe · Equipe de Graphistes · Pentagram

Client · Auftraggeber · Client · I.R.M. Magazine

| Information Technology Brochure. Water-colour and crayon | Informations-Technologie Broschüre Wasserfarben und Farbstifte | Technologie de l'information Brochure. Aquarelle et pastel |

Designer · Gestalter · Maquettiste · Jim Allen and Philip Evans

Design Group · Design Gruppe · Equipe de Graphistes · The Jim Allen Design Team Limited

| Change of Address Card. Scraperboard in black and white | Karte zur Bekanntgebung einer neuen Adresse. Schabtechnik in schwarz-weiß | Carte de changement d'adresse. Carte grattage en noir et blanc |

Art Director · Kunstredakteur · Redacteur Artistique · Marcello Minale

Designer · Gestalter · Maquettiste · Jeff Willis

Design Group · Design Gruppe · Equipe de Graphistes · Minale, Tattersfield & Partners Limited

Client · Auftraggeber · Client · Harrods Limited

Symbol for packaging and French merchandise for Harrods department store. Magic markers	Symbol für Verpackung und französische Waren für Harrods. Magic markers	Symbole d'emballage et de marchandise française pour le magasin Harrods. Magic markers

Art Director · Kunstredakteur · Redacteur Artistique · Jean-Christian Knaff

Designer · Gestalter · Maquettiste · Richard Parent

Client · Auftraggeber · Client · Belugas Productions Montreal

Favourite Songs	Lieblingslieder	Les Chants aimés
Record Cover.	Plattenhülle.	Enveloppe de disque.
Water-colour and mixed media	Wasserfarben und Mischtechnik	Aquarelle et moyens divers

Designer · Gestalter · Maquettiste · Virginia Armstrong

Design Group · Design Gruppe · Equipe de Graphistes · Fitch & Company

Fitch Christmas Party	Einladung zur Fitch	Invitation à la Fête de Noël
Invitation.	Weihnachtsparty.	de Fitch.
Collage and water-colour	Collage und Wasserfarben	Collage et aquarelle

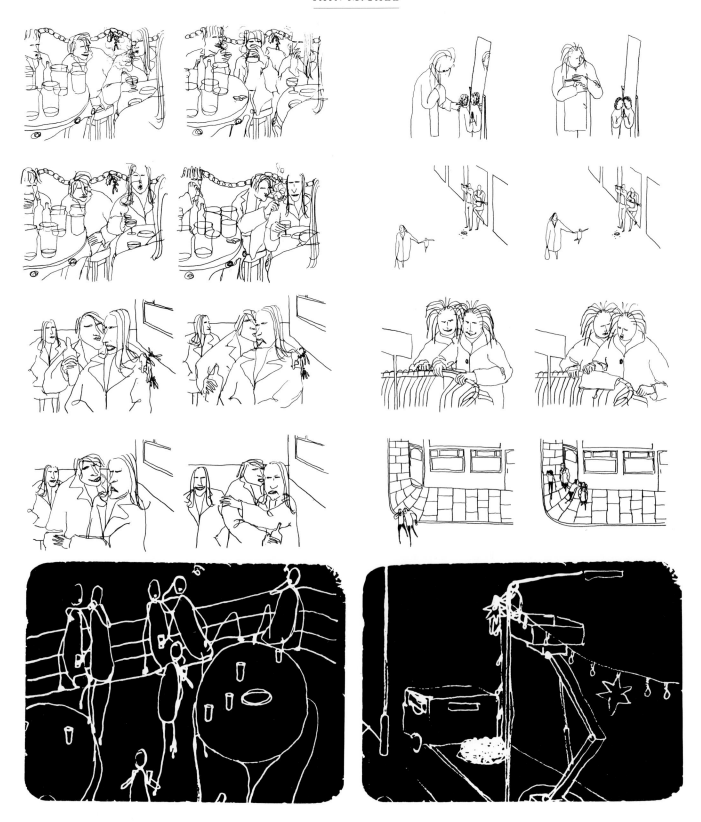

Animator · Trickfilmzeichner · Dessinateur de Films d'Animation · Iain McCall

Editor · Cutter · Monteur · Iain McCall

Rostrum Camera · Rostrum Kamera · Camera du Rostre · Iain McCall

Production Company · Produktionsgesellschaft · Compagnie de Productions · Liverpool Polytechnic

Christmas for Sale	Weihnachten zum Verkauf	Noël à vendre
Animated film to Ravel	Trickfilm mit Musik von Ravel	Film d'animation sur musique de Ravel

Animator · Trickfilmzeichner · Dessinateur de Films d'Animation · Susan Young

Editor · Cutter · Monteur · Susan Young

Rostrum Camera · Rostrum Kamera · Camera du Rostre · Susan Young

Music Composer · Arranger · Musik · Musique · Carl Washington

Production Company · Produktionsgesellschaft · Compagnie de Productions · Royal College of Art Film School

Carnival   Karneval   Carnaval

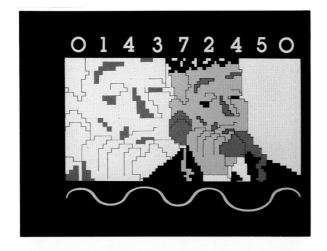

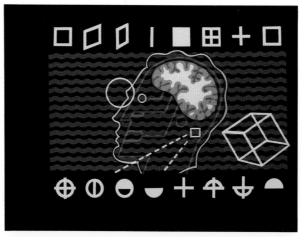

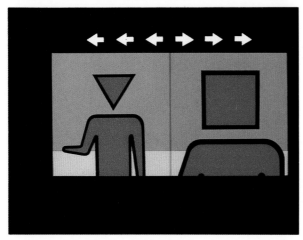

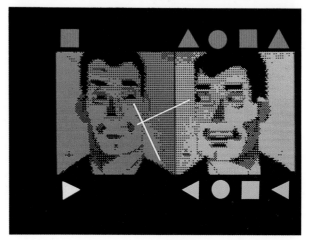

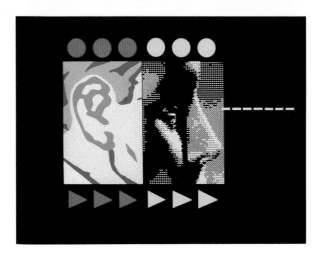

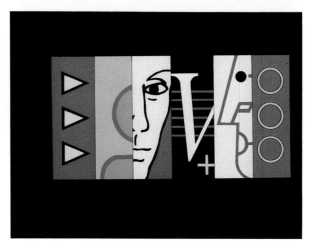

Animator · Trickfilmzeichner · Dessinateur de Films d'Animation · Bob Lawrie		
Director · Regisseur · Réalisteur · Bob Lawrie		
Rostrum Camera · Rostrum Kamera · Camera du Rostre · Begonia Tamarit		
Music Composer · Musik · Musique · Peter Griffiths		
Agency Producer · Agentur-Produzent · Producteur · Paul Harvey		
Advertising Agency · Werbeagentur · Agence de Publicite · One Point Five Limited		
Production Company · Produktionsgesellschaft · Compagnie de Productions · Blink Productions		
Client · Auftraggeber · Client · Investors in Industry		
Relationships	Beziehungen	Relations

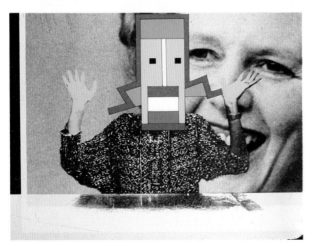

Animator · Trickfilmzeichner · Dessinateur de Films d'Animation · Bob Lawrie

Editor · Cutter · Monteur · Charlotte Evans

Director · Regisseur · Réalisteur · Bob Lawrie

Rostrum Camera · Rostrum Kamera · Camera du Rostre · Julian Holdaway

Agency Producer · Agentur-Produzent · Producteur · Pat Gavin

Production Company · Produktionsgesellschaft · Compagnie de Productions · Blink Productions

Client · Auftraggeber · Client · London Weekend Television

| Around Midnight | Um Mitternacht | Autour de minuit |

 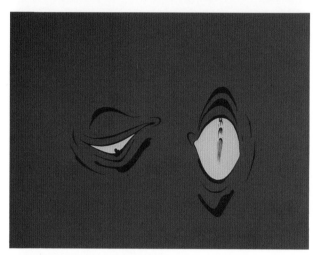

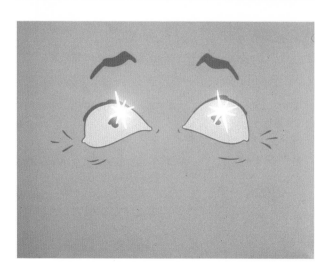 

Animator · Trickfilmzeichner · Dessinateur de Films d'Animation · Greg Millar		
Editor · Cutter · Monteur · Andrew Gillman		
Director · Regisseur · Réalisteur · Rocky Morton and Annabel Jankel		
Music Composer · Musik · Musique · Dennis King		
Agency Producer · Agentur-Produzent · Producteur · Rachel Perry		
Advertising Agency · Werbeagentur · Agence de Publicite · T.B.W.A.		
Production Company · Produktionsgesellschaft · Compagnie de Productions · Cucumber Studios		
Client · Auftraggeber · Client · Dunlopillo Division U.K.		
Rusty Bedsprings	Verrostete Sprungfedern	Ressorts de lit rouillés

Animator · Trickfilmzeichner · Dessinateur de Films d'Animation · Tony White and Richard Burdett		
Editor · Cutter · Monteur · John Carey		
Copywriter · Texter · Redacteur · Pete Hopkins		
Director · Regisseur · Réalisteur · Steve Nanson		
Rostrum Camera · Rostrum Kamera · Camera du Rostre · Roy Lacey		
Music Arranger · Musik · Musique · Richard Myhill		
Agency Producer · Agentur-Produzent · Producteur · Jo Moore		
Advertising Agency · Werbeagentur · Agence de Publicite · Aspect Advertising		
Production Company · Produktionsgesellschaft · Compagnie de Productions · The Animation Partnership		
Client · Auftraggeber · Client · Potterton International		
This Ole House	This Ole House	This Ole House

CITROËN 2CV £2674.

[*FAITHFULUS RELIABUS*]

Animator · Trickfilmzeichner · Dessinateur de Films d'Animation · Peter Brookes

Copywriter · Texter · Rédacteur · Steve Hooper

Director · Regisseur · Réalisteur · Dennis Lewis

Agency Producer · Agentur-Produzent · Producteur · Pauline Crane

Advertising Agency · Werbeagentur · Agence de Publicite · Colman RSCG & Partners

Client · Auftraggeber · Client · Citroen Cars Limited

Tortoise	Schildkröte	Tortue

Animator · Trickfilmzeichner · Dessinateur de Films d'Animation · Joanne Rodmilovich

Designer · Gestalter · Maquettiste · Jim Downie

Director · Regisseur · Réalisteur · Will Vinton

Agency Producer · Agentur-Produzent · Producteur · David McCowan-Hill

Advertising Agency · Werbeagentur · Agence de Publicite · Crawford Halls (Edinburgh)

Production Company · Produktionsgesellschaft · Compagnie de Productions · Will Vinton Productions

Client · Auftraggeber · Client · Scotsman Publications

Changing Character   Die Wandlung des Charakters   Transmutation

Art Director · Art Direktor · Directeur Artistique Mike McGann		
Animator · Trickfilmzeichner · Dessinateur de Films d'Animation · Oscar Grillo		
Editor · Cutter · Monteur · Charlotte Evans		
Director · Regisseur · Réalisteur · Oscar Grillo		
Copywriter · Texter · Rédacteur · Chips Hardy		
Music Arranger · Musik · Musique · Paul Hart and Joe Campbell		
Agency Producer · Agentur-Produzent · Producteur · Jean Rayment		
Advertising Agency · Werbeagentur · Agence de Publicite · Dorland Advertising Limited		
Production Company · Produktionsgesellschaft · Compagnie de Productions · Klactoveesedstene Animations Limited		
Client · Auftraggeber · Client · Daily Telegraph		
Frogs	Frösche	Grenouilles

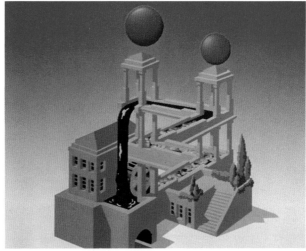

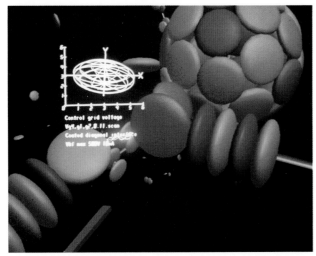

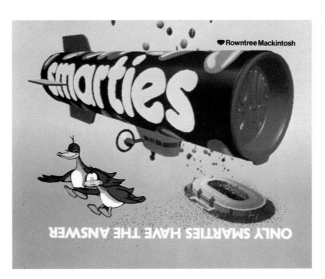

Animator · Trickfilmzeichner · Dessinateur de Films d'Animation · Martin Lambie-Nairn
Jilly Knight (Computer)

Designer · Gestalter · Maquettiste · Billy Mawhinney

Director · Regisseur · Réalisateur · Martin Lambie-Nairn

Editor · Cutter · Monteur · John Carey

Copywriter · Texter · Rédacteur · Nick Welch

Music Composer · Musik · Musique · Paul Caplan

Agency Producer · Agentur-Produzent · Producteur · Simon Wells

Advertising Agency · Werbeagentur · Agence de Publicite · J. Walter Thompson Company Limited

Production Company · Produktionsgesellschaft · Compagnie de Productions · Robinson Lambie-Nairn

Client · Auftraggeber · Client · Rowntree Mackintosh plc

| Get Smarties | Smarties kaufen | Procurez-vous des Smarties |

Background Artist · Hintergrundmaler · Warren Madill	
Animator · Trickfilmzeichner · Dessinateur de Films d'Animation · Matt Forrest and Greg Millar	
Editor · Cutter · Monteur · Peter Hearn and Tony Fish	
Director · Regisseur · Réalisateur · Matt Forrest	
Rostrum Camera · Rostrum Kamera · Camera du Rostre · Matt Forrest	
Copywriter · Texter · Rédacteur · Steve Henry	
Art Director · Art Direktor · Directeur Artistique · Axel Chaldecott	
Agency Producer · Agentur-Produzent · Producteur · Diane Croll	
Advertising Agency · Werbeagentur · Agence de Publicite · Gold Greenlees Trott	
Production Company · Produktionsgesellschaft · Compagnie de Productions · Big Features	
Client · Auftraggeber · Client · Taunton Autumn Gold Cider	

Haywain	Heuwagen	Charrette à foin

Background Artist · Hintergrundmaler · Dessinateur d'arrière plan · Warren Maddil		
Animator · Trickfilmzeichner · Dessinateur de Films d'Animation · Matt Forrest and Greg Millar		
Editor · Cutter · Monteur · Peter Hearn and Tony Fish		
Director · Regisseur · Réalisateur · Matt Forrest		
Rostrum Camera · Rostrum Kamera · Camera du Rostre · Matt Forrest		
Copywriter · Texter · Rédacteur · Steve Henry		
Art Director · Art Direktor · Directeur Artistique · Axel Chaldecott		
Agency Producer · Agentur-Produzent · Producteur · Diane Croll		
Advertising Agency · Werbeagentur · Agence de Publicite · Gold Greenlees Trott		
Production Company · Produktionsgesellschaft · Compagnie de Productions · Big Features		
Client · Auftraggeber · Client · Taunton Autumn Gold Cider		
Viaduct	Viadukt	Viaduc

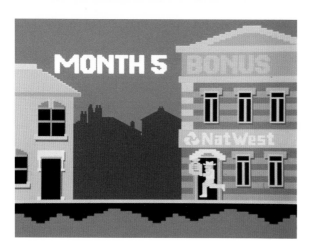

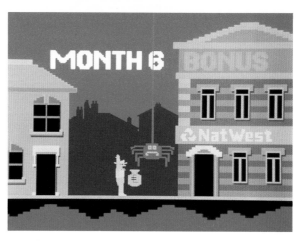

Animator · Trickfilmzeichner · Dessinateur de Films d'Animation · Ken Brown		
Chris Briscoe (Computer)		
Peter Florence (Computer)		
Editor · Cutter · Monteur · Neil Mills		
Director · Regisseur · Réalisateur · Ken Brown		
Designer · Gestalter · Maquettiste · Tom Moult		
Copywriter · Texter · Rédacteur · Nick Welch		
Music Composer · Musik · Musique · Hans Zimmer		
Agency Producer · Agentur-Produzent · Producteur · Bill Hammond and Simon Wells		
Advertising Agency · Werbeagentur · Agence de Publicite · J. Walter Thompson Company Limited		
Production Company · Produktionsgesellschaft · Compagnie de Productions · Directors Studio		
Client · Auftraggeber · Client · National Westminster Bank plc		
Bank Man	Bank Mann	Homme de banque

Animator · Trickfilmzeichner · Dessinateur de Films d'Animation · Michael Stuart	
Designer · Gestalter · Maquettiste · Jill Brooks	
Editor · Cutter · Monteur · Greg Willcox and Peter Hearn	
Director · Regisseur · Réalisateur · Brian Byfield, Tony May, Michael Stuart	
Copywriter · Texter · Rédacteur · Alfredo Marcantonio	
Rostrum Camera · Rostrum Kamera · Camera du Rostre · Geoff Axtell	
Music Arranger · Musik · Musique · Paul Hart and Joe Campbell	
Agency Producer · Agentur-Produzent · Producteur · Erika Issitt	
Advertising Agency · Werbeagentur · Agence de Publicite · Lowe Howard-Spink Campbell-Ewald	
Production Company · Produktionsgesellschaft · Compagnie de Productions · J. R. Stuart Brooks Animation/ Park Village Productions/Brian Byfield Films	
Client · Auftraggeber · Client · Whitbread & Company Limited	

Jack the Lad	Jack, der Kerl	Le joueur au valet

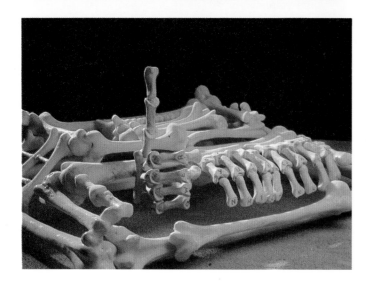

Animator · Trickfilmzeichner · Dessinateur de Films d'Animation · Peter Lord

Editor · Cutter · Monteur · John Merritt

Designer · Gestalter · Maquettiste · Richard (Golly) Goleszowski

Director · Regisseur · Réalisateur · Peter Lord and David Sproxton

Copywriter · Texter · Rédacteur · Mike Stephenson

Music Arranger · Musik · Musique · Joe Campbell and Paul Hart

Agency Producer · Agentur-Produzent · Producteur · Annie Alexander

Advertising Agency · Werbeagentur · Agence de Publicité · Lowe Howard-Spink Campbell-Ewald

Production Company · Produktionsgesellschaft · Compagnie de Productions · Aardman Animation

Client · Auftraggeber · Client · Enterprise Computers

| Dem Bones | Dem Bones | Ces vieux os |

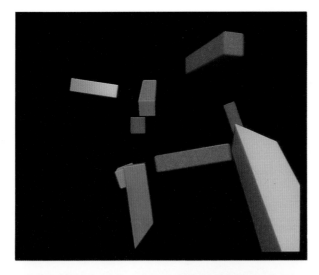 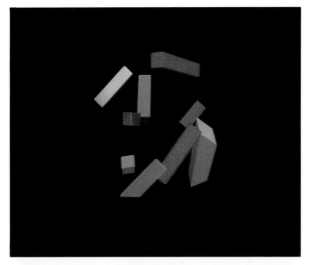

 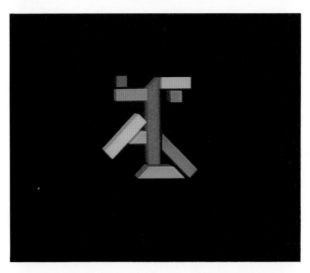

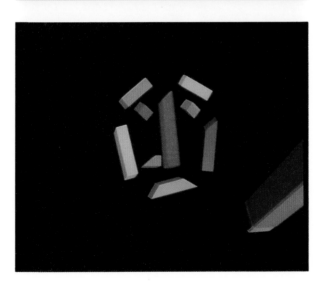 

Hamlet. The mild cigar.

Animator · Trickfilmzeichner · Dessinateur de Films d'Animation · Graham Ralph
Tony Ford (Computer)

Editor · Cutter · Monteur · (Film) John Carey
(Video) Nigel Hadley

Director · Regisseur · Réalisateur · Anna Hart and Martin Lambie-Nairn

Designer · Gestalter · Maquettiste · Anna Hart

Art Director · Art Direktor · Directeur Artistique · Rod Waskett

Copywriter · Texter · Rédacteur · Paul Weinberger

Music Arranger · Musik · Musique · Paul Hart and Joe Campbell

Agency Producer · Agentur-Produzent · Producteur · Alec Ovens

Advertising Agency · Werbeagentur · Agence de Publicite · Collett Dickenson Pearce & Partners

Production Company · Produktionsgesellschaft · Compagnie de Productions · Robinson Lambie-Nairn

Client · Auftraggeber · Client · Gallaher Limited

Hamlet Channel 5   Hamlet Channel 5   Hamlet Chaîne 5

Animator · Trickfilmzeichner · Dessinateur de Films d'Animation · Nigel Mairs

Editor · Cutter · Monteur · Nigel Mairs

Rostrum Camera · Rostrum Kamera · Camera du Rostre · Nigel Mairs and Ian Cole

Music Composer · Musik · Musique · Jon Williams

Production Company · Produktionsgesellschaft · Compagnie de Productions · Liverpool Polytechnic

| Reflection | Reflektierung | Reflexion |

Animator · Trickfilmzeichner · Dessinateur de Films d'Animation · Geoff Dunbar		
Editor · Cutter · Monteur · Peter Hearn and Tony Fish		
Director · Regisseur · Réalisateur · Geoff Dunbar		
Rostrum Camera · Rostrum Kamera · Camera du Rostre · Gary Knowlden and Richard Wolf		
Music Composer · Musik · Musique · Paul McCartney		
Production Company · Produktionsgesellschaft · Compagnie de Productions · MPL Communications Limited/ Grand Slam Animation		
We All Stand Together	Wir stehen alle beisammen	Nous nous tenons tous

Collection of George Hardie

A Homage to Tintin
For the Miro Gallery,
Barcelona.
Ink and collage

Eine Huldigung Tintins
Für die Miro Gallerie,
Barzelona.
Tusche und Collage

Un hommage à Tintin
pour la galerie Miro à
Barcelone.
Encre et collage

The Extraordinary Bird	Der ausserordentliche Vogel	L'oiseau extraordinaire
From a series of prints and drawings,	Aus einer Reihe von Drucken und Zeichnungen	D'une série de gravures et dessins,
Boys and Birds, illustrating a fable.	Boys and Birds zur Illustration einer Fabel.	Garçons et Oiseaux, illustrant une fable.
Lino cut	Linolschnitt	Gravure sur lino

Seven Sisters
Idea for a tube poster.
Crayon

Seven Sisters
Idee für ein Plakat für die
Untergrundbahn.
Farbstifte

Seven Sisters
Idée pour une affiche de métro.
Pastel

June
Handmade calendar.
Oil pastels

Juni
Ein handgemachter Kalender.
Ölpastell

Juin
Calendrier fait main.
Pastels à l'huile

Painter
Portfolio.
Water-colour and conté pencil

Maler
Portfolio.
Wasserfarben und Conté-Stifte

Peintre
Portfolio.
Aquarelle et crayon conté

Corkscrew Hairstyle
Water-colour

Korkenzieher-Haar.
Wasserfarben

Coiffure tire-bouchon
Aquarelle

From a series of works
for a one man exhibition
at the Scottish Amicable
building,
Glasgow in February 1985.
Pastel

Aus einer Reihe von Arbeiten
für eine Einzelausstellung
im Gebäude der Scottish
Amicable,
Glasgow im Februar 1985.
Pastellfarben

D'une série d'oeuvres pour une
exposition d'un seul artiste
au bâtiment de la Scottish
Amicable,
Glasgow en février 1985.
Pastel

Heart of the Town
Portfolio.
Water-colour

Das Herz der Stadt
Portfolio.
Wasserfarben

Le Coeur de la Ville
Portfolio.
Aquarelle

Publisher · Verlag · Editeur · Unique Images Limited

The Old Man and the Sea	Der alte Mann und das Meer	Le Vieil Homme et la Mer
Greetings Card.	Grußkarte.	Carte de voeux.
Water-colour	Wasserfarben	Aquarelle

Hippo Escaping From the Zoo
For a children's story
written by the artist.
Water-colour and pencil

Nilpferd auf der Flucht aus
dem Zoo
Für eine Kindergeschichte
des Künstlers.
Wasserfarben und Bleistift

Hippopotame s'échappant
du Zoo
Pour une histoire pour enfants
écrite par l'artiste.
Aquarelle et crayon

Stepping Out
Portfolio.
Chalk pastel

Ausgehen
Portfolio.
Kreide-Pastell

Sortir
Portfolio.
Pastel de craie

Happy Cat Before
the Evolution
of Human Civilization
Ink and crayon

Glückliche Katze vor
der Evolution
der menschlichen Zivilisation.
Tusche und Farbstifte

Chat heureux avant l'évolution
de la
civilisation humaine.
Encre et pastel

Art Director · Art Direktor · Directeur Artistique · Derek Ungless

Calvi, a Hanged Man
Commissioned but not
published by Rolling Stone.
Water-colour

Calvi, der hingerichtete Mann
Beauftragt von Rolling Stone
aber nicht veröffentlicht.
Wasserfarben

Calvi, homme pendu
Commandé mais non publié
par Rolling Stone.
Aquarelle

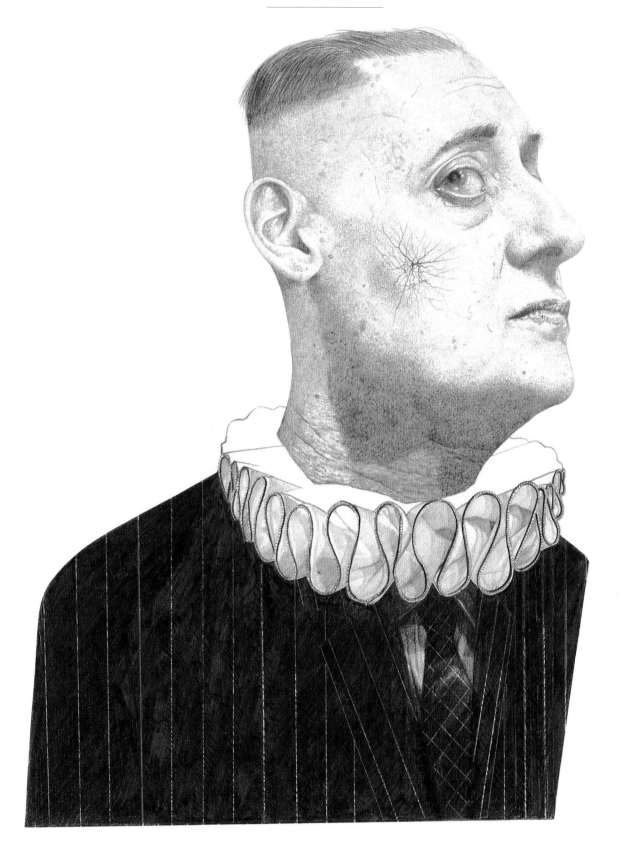

The Man Who Could Only
Quote Shakespeare
Portfolio.
Pencil and inks

Der Mann, der nur Shakespeare
zitieren konnte
Portfolio.
Bleistift und Tusche

L'homme qui ne pouvait que
citer Shakespeare
Portfolio.
Crayon et encres

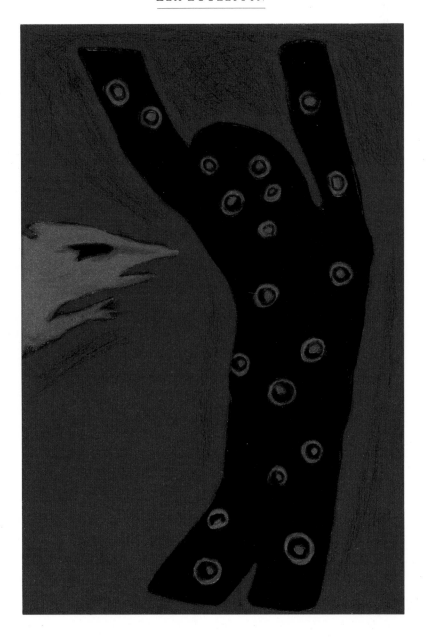

If Matisse Saw the Plague in
His Later Years
Intended as the cover
of a paperback
The Plague, unpublished.
Gouache, crayon and pencil

Wenn Matisse die Pest in
seinen späteren Jahren
gesehen hätte
Beauftragt als Titel eines
Taschenbuchs
The Plague, unveröffentlicht.
Gouache, Farbstifte und
Bleistift

Si Matisse a vu la peste dans ses
dernières années
Destiné à la couverture
d'un livre de poche
La Peste, non publié.
Gouache, pastel et crayon

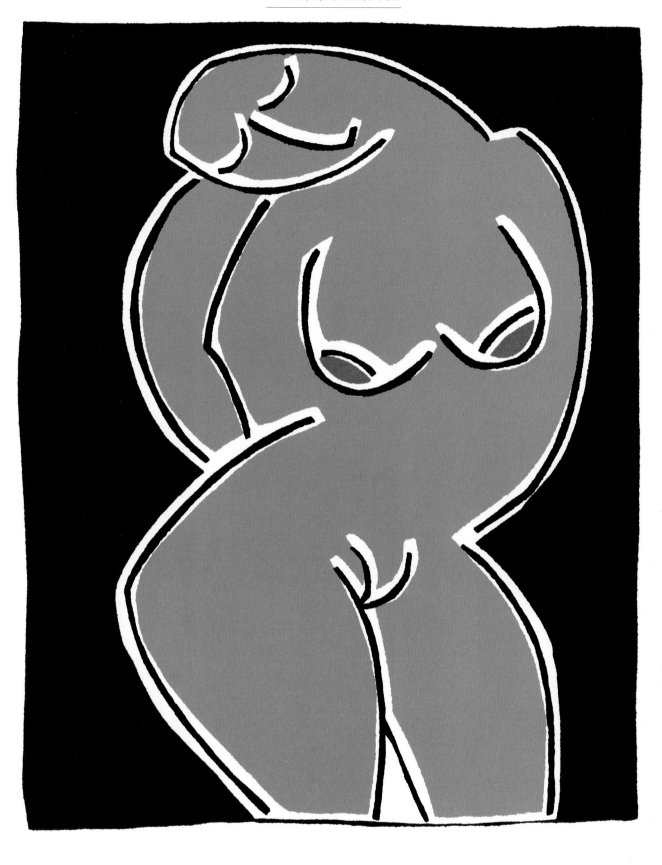

The Venus in June	Venus im Juni	La Venus en juin
Student portfolio.	Portfolio eines Studenten.	Portfolio d'étudiant.
Screenprint	Siebdruck	Sérigraphie

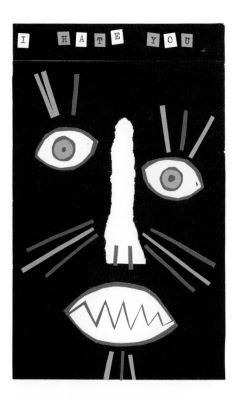

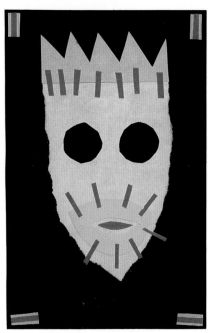

Passmore-People
College project.
Coloured paper collage

Passmore-Leute
College-Projekt.
Farbige Papier-Collage

Les gens de Passmore
Projet de college
Collage de papiers de couleur

Passmore-People
College project.
Coloured paper collage

Passmore-Leute
College-Projekt.
Farbige Papier-Collage

Les gens de Passmore
Projet de college
Collage de papiers de couleur

WE ARE HAPPY WE HAVE POOHPIE ™

WE ARE HAPPY WE HAVE KAKBAR ™

Passmore-People
College project.
Coloured paper collage

Passmore-Leute
College-Projekt.
Farbige Papier-Collage

Les gens de Passmore
Projet de college
Collage de papiers de couleur

NEW

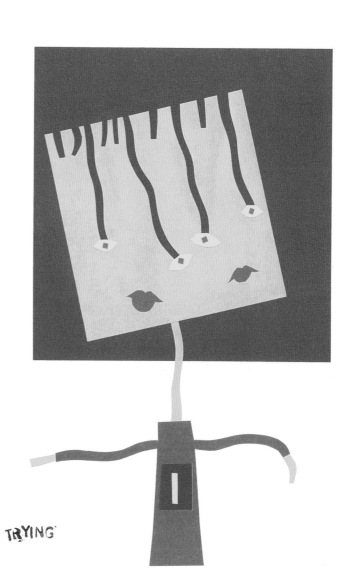

TRYING

Passmore-People
College project.
Coloured paper collage

Passmore-Leute
College-Projekt.
Farbige Papier-Collage

Les gens de Passmore
Projet de college
Collage de papiers de couleur

Conflict
Personal project on
Aborigonal art
and mythology.
Coloured pencils

Konflikt
Eine eigene Arbeit über die
Kunst und
Mythologie der Ureinwohner.
Farbstifte

Conflit
Etude personnelle sur l'art et la
mythologie aborigènes.
Crayons de couleur

It's Not Disneyland, Folks
Personal project from an article
in the New York Times
entitled
Nuclear Energy –
Wheat or Chaff?
Pen and ink

Es ist nicht Disneyland, Leute
Eine eigene Arbeit aus
einem Artikel
in The New York Times
mit dem Titel
Kernenergie –
Weizen oder Spreu?
Feder und Tusche

Ce n'est pas le Disneyland,
les amis
Projet personnel d'un article
dans The New York Times
intitulé
Energie nucléaire –
bon grain ou ivraie?
Plume et encre

The Woodland Floor
in Autumn
College project for a book on
country walks through the
seasons.
Water-colour

Der Waldboden im Herbst
College-Projekt für ein
Buch über
Wanderungen in
verschiedenen Jahreszeiten.
Wasserfarben

Le sol des bois à l'automne
Etude de collège pour un livre
sur les promenades à la
campagne à travers les saisons.
Aquarelle

ARTISTS

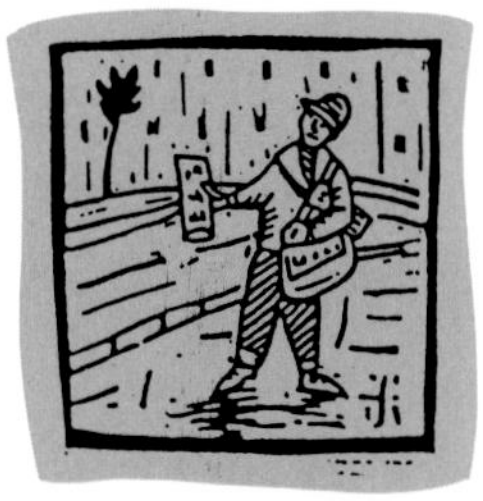

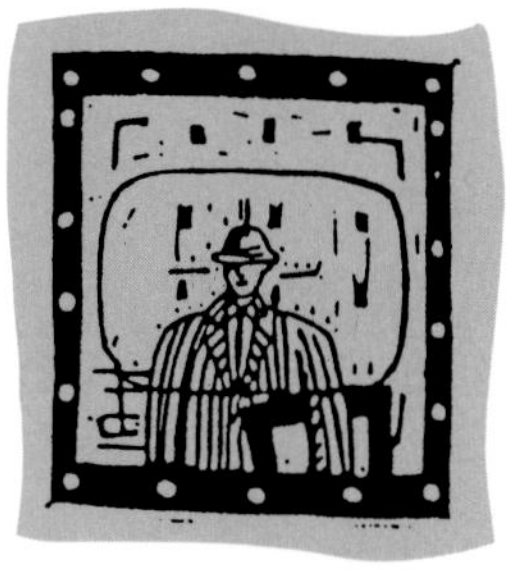

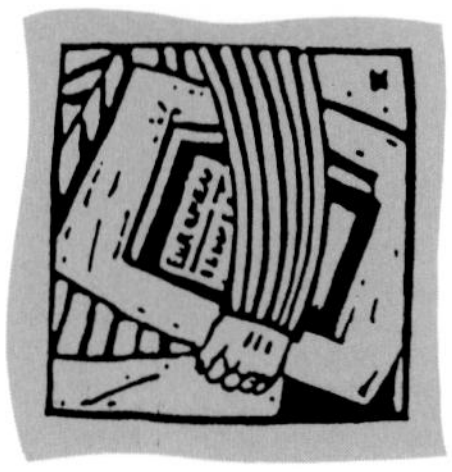